Mark Kauffman created a
painterly effect backlighting
a solitary punter gliding
down the Thames.

Photographing Sports: John Zimmerman, Mark Kauffman and Neil Leifer

text by Sean Callahan and Gerald Astor
with the editors of Alskog, Inc.

Prepared by Alskog, Inc.
Lawrence Schiller / Publisher
William Hopkins / Design Director
John Poppy / Executive Editor
Sean Callahan / Editorial Coordinator
Ira Fast / Production Manager
Julie Asher Palladino / Design Assistant
Judith R. Schiller / Copy Editor
Lou Jacobs, Jr. / Technical Editor

An Alskog Book
published with
Thomas Y. Crowell Company, Inc.

Photographs copyright © 1975 by John Zimmerman, Mark Kauffman, and Neil Leifer
Photographs previously copyrighted by John Zimmerman, Mark Kauffman, and Neil Leifer
Text copyright © 1975 by Sean Callahan and Gerald Astor and Alskog, Inc.
Technical section text copyright © 1975 Lou Jacobs, Jr.

Alskog, Inc., 9200 Sunset Boulevard, Suite 1001
Los Angeles, California, 90069

Library of Congress Catalog Card Number: 75-12965
ISBN 0-690-00786-8 Soft cover
ISBN 0-690-00785-X Hard cover

First Printing
Published simultaneously in Canada

Printed in the United States of America

Zimmerman amplified the
fury of the pack with well-
placed electronic flash.

4

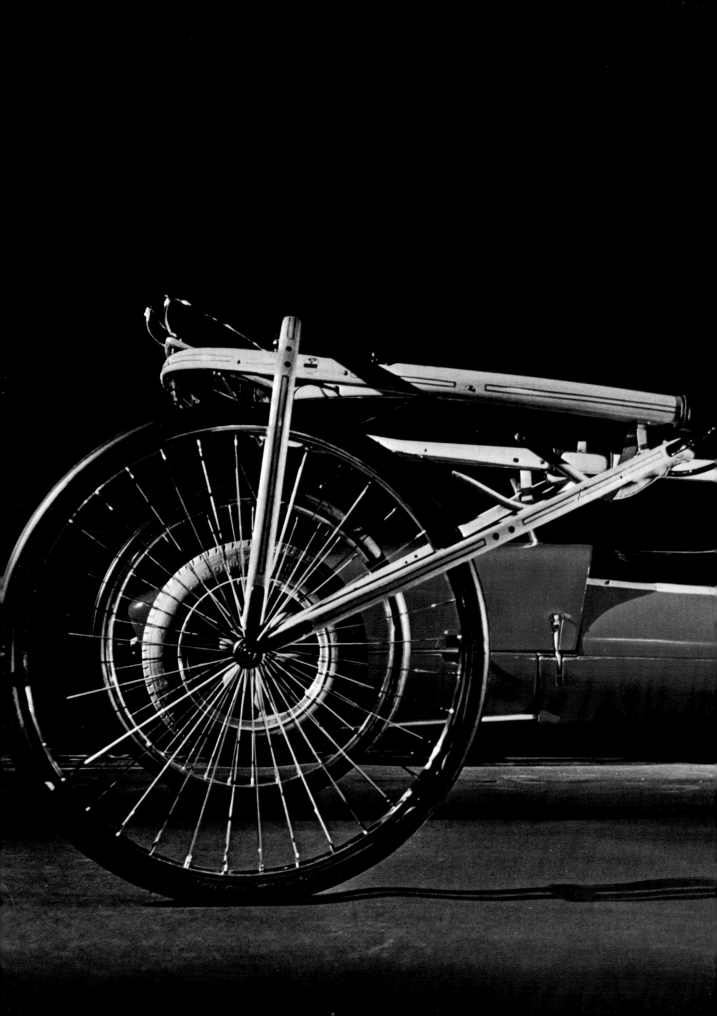

Kauffman's eye for design
telescoped the wheels of
two classic racers.

Introduction

From the beginning, photographers have been fascinated with the concept of people in motion. Daguerre's 1839 photograph of a Parisian boulevard at first seemed deserted. A surprised Samuel F. B. Morse, the father of American photography, described it as "so constantly filled with a moving throng of pedestrians and carriages [that it was] perfectly solitary." The long exposure time had failed to record anything that moved. Motion photography was then, as today, inexorably wedded to the developing technology of the medium.

With improved photographic processes, exposure times came down, allowing for higher shutter speeds. The camera itself, however, was an inhibiting factor. Because of its huge size, it was mounted on a tripod and largely confined to the studio. Thus evolved a concept of photography that limited it to portraits, still lifes and landscapes.

In 1874 horse fancier Leland Stanford hired photographer Eadweard Muybridge to prove in pictures his assumption that at one instant in the stride all of a horse's hooves were off the ground. Muybridge had the horse pass in front of a battery of 12 cameras that resulted in the first true photo sequence, but the success of the experiment was due to an electromagnetic shutter capable of 1/1000 second exposures.

Faster shutters, better lenses and the popularization of the medium through the introduction of roll film cameras by George Eastman in 1886 allowed for more experimentation with motion. Yet by the end of World War I, when the technology enabled photographers to effortlessly freeze the moment, they were content to stop there. For nearly 50 years sports photography was mired in the backwaters of the medium. The favored camera, up into the sixties, was a unit consisting of a 4x5 (or larger) Graflex attached to a gargantuan telephoto lens that had to be caged in a special press gallery far from the action. When Mark Kauffman walked onto the field with a specially adapted sequence camera, a new era in sports photography began. His colleague, John Zimmerman, would later refine the instrument and couple it with innovative lighting concepts. Observing their progress from the sideline was Neil Leifer, an aspiring young amateur unfettered by cumbersome cameras, whose vision matured along with the increasing sophistication of the 35mm single-lens reflex system. He eventually became one of its modern masters.

This portrait of three photographers owes much of its strength to the generous help of their fellow professionals John Dominis, Walter Iooss, Jr., and writers Gerry Cooke; Coles Phinizy and John Frook; Erla Frank Zwingle; and of course John Zimmerman, Mark Kauffman, Neil Leifer and their families.

Neil Leifer turned the grandstands into a graphic device for this familiar pose of Willie Mays.

Flying high overhead, Leifer noticed the contrast between idling paddlers and a streaking surfer.

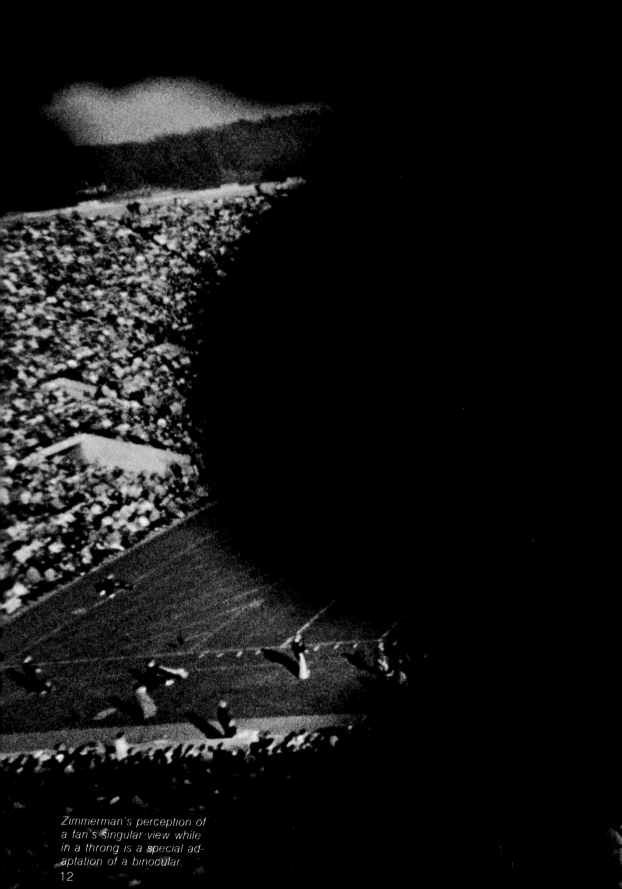

Zimmerman's perception of
a fan's singular view while
in a throng is a special ad-
aptation of a binocular.

Sharing the Life of the Hero

The work of sports photographers is unique in that it compels us to look again at what we have seen before and know to be true. The game is familiar to all. The rules never change, the costumes are familiar, the route to victory is clear. Only the inevitable result is in doubt.

Yet, in an era when more and more prime time television hours beam sport to millions, over two million people turn to *Sports Illustrated* magazine a week after the event to see how Mark Kauffman, John Zimmerman, Neil Leifer and their colleagues saw it. Sports pages sell many more million newspapers every day, especially when there is nothing more newsworthy on the front page. Smart editors of tabloids give sport photographs big play on the back page, where the reader automatically begins his perusal of the paper.

Among photojournalists, those who best embody the romance and panache of the medium are those roguish recorders of men at war. Standing next to them, but not in their shadow, are the recorders of man in motion. While the combat photographer hints at the possibility of imminent death, the sports photographer celebrates the vitality of life. Their subjects constantly push themselves to new heights. Athletes are heroes who nearly always live another day to do battle with their adversaries, themselves, the elements, or the clock.

Capturing the exhilaration of sport is the special province of a specialized photographer. The sports photographer is very often just an overgrown fan. He had all the savvy for the sport, but couldn't muster up the requisite height or pare off the excess weight to make the team. So he occupies that nether world along the sidelines that makes him part voyeur, part participant. To the envy of those of us in the stands, the sports photographer often has the best seat in the house. He is so close to the action that he sometimes becomes part of it, like when a scampering halfback gets blown out of bounds by a thundering linebacker who, in the process, cleans out a nest of sideline photographers. Sports photographers have the sagacity of seasoned coaches in knowing what the next move will be, or should be, so as to anticipate the action. They have the rat-like cunning of a hustler in maneuvering themselves or their cameras into the proper position. Handling the petty officials like guards and ushers that keep us mortals at bay may require tools as important to the photographer as his telephoto lens or motor-driven camera. They include such devices as cool professionalism, ego massage, arrogant bluster and downright bribery.

The sports photographer is permitted to slap the butt of the hero and nod condolences to the goat. He drinks in the smells of liniment, adhesive tape, matted turf and hard-earned sweat. He shares in the athletes' locker room camaraderie, their sideline tensions, their private solitudes. His spirits soar with the swooshing downhill racer and still to the intense concentration of the balance-beam gymnast. His position makes him quiver at the deliverance of a tattoo of combination punches, and recoil with a knockout blow. He gasps at the sight of a tire-squealing spinout, and his heart seizes when the car disintegrates into a fiery ball of gasoline, metal shards and errant wheels neatly snapped from their axles careening wildly about the track like billiard balls fleeing a fierce break shot. Training and instinct keeps his eye fixed to the viewfinder, his finger furiously working the shutter button, recording every horrible detail while you and I, safely in the stands or at home behind the screen, wince with horror and perhaps cover our faces.

Sports photographers are the primary witnesses to those events. They spot the epochal moment in a fraction of a second, and fix it forever on film before a Howard Cosell up in the booth drones out the obvious to the rest of us with a generous assist from the slow-motion replay. Yet, for all the glam-

John G. Zimmerman, with his pipe and Hulcher camera.

our and the glory, few of us are aware of the toil, angst and ignominy that often accompanies these professionals. Seldom told are the hours spent rigging the lights in an auditorium only to have an inexpensive photocell short out just before game time. Runaway strobe lights turn the hall into a crazed discothèque that irritates fans, infuriates players, and slaps a ban on all photographers from ever entering that hall with so much as a penlight for the rest of time. There are days when the photographer is stranded on the back nine with the favorite while the tournament's dark horse eagles the 18th hole for the championship. And although they occupy the most privileged seats at a spectator sport, because they are journalists first, they are so swept up by the story to be told that they seldom get to enjoy the game itself.

Sport is often called a microcosm of life, and so too is sports photography a microcosm of all the other forms of the medium. It allows for documentary expression, studio wizardry, and mass communication. The three men in this volume are among the best exponents of the various facets of sports photography. They have a facility with all areas, but have a dominant strength in one that sets them apart from their colleagues.

Mark Kauffman is the quiet, sensitive photo essayist. His elegant pictorialism in portraying punting on the Thames (page 1) bespeaks the refinement of English sporting life. His studio treatment of two sporting vehicles (pages 6–7) is rich in symbolism.

John Zimmerman is a brilliant, sophisticated

Mark Kauffman during the coverage of a UCLA football game.

photo technician. He pushes the technology of the medium to its limits, and when that's not enough, rolls it back even further with devices of his own design that give the reader an unparalleled view of sports. We are in the midst of an explosive pack of greyhounds one instant (pages 4–5), hovering high over snowy peaks with a hang-glider the next (pages 2–3), or channeled inside a pair of binoculars at a football game (pages 12–13).

Neil Leifer is the energetic, versatile sports photographer. Once a generation behind his predecessors at *Sports Illustrated,* he drew upon their experiences and techniques until he emerged as their peer. He evokes rousing emotions in a classic performance by Willie Mays (pages 8–9) and imaginative vision by shooting from a platform in the sky hovering above surfers (pages 10–11). Emotion and technology

deftly employed make Leifer the quintessential photojournalist, the precocious star of the magazine's staff, and an excellent model for the emerging sports photographer.

Mark Kauffman: An Eye for Emotion

Mark Kauffman was born in 1922, the son of a Los Angeles blacksmith who was still shoeing horses throughout the twenties. From the beginning he demonstrated the enterprise and imagination necessary for a career in photojournalism. When he was 14, a truck capsized

near the Kauffman home. Mark ran to borrow a neighbor's camera, a folding Kodak. The truck's cargo of tomatoes had spilled all over the street. Realizing he could not get an effective picture from ground level, he scampered up a telephone pole for elevation, took his shots, then grabbed a streetcar to the *Los Angeles Examiner.* They paid $5 for the picture and ran it across a full page, eight columns wide.

"Photography was magic—press a button and produce a picture. That hooked me," says Kauffman. "You were a kind of sorcerer, standing in the dim red glow of the darkroom and summoning a print to life in the chemical tray. I also saw in photography a way to become a traveler, to roam the world, to be in the middle of exciting events."

His first camera was an Argus C3, the first popular 35mm for the advanced amateur. His father sold Mark's clarinet to make the down payment. With this new camera Kauffman produced his first sports picture at a school track meet. Instead of standing to one side while the runners approached the finish line, he shot them head-on. "I wasn't sure that my shutter speed would be fast enough to stop the action, (1/300 second was the Argus's fastest) and I had heard that from straight on, photographing action was less of a problem. Besides, everybody photographed from the sidelines, and I wanted something different."

In Los Angeles at the time Kauffman was growing up, a rare experiment in photography came to fruition, and from it would emerge the greatest concentration of photojournalistic talent the medium has yet to see. Clarence A. Bach, a teacher at John C. Fremont High School, had convinced authorities in the late twenties to add an intensive course in photography to the vocational training curriculum. The course became a full-scale class with three hours of lab and field work plus an hour of classroom instruction every day.

Bach and another instructor tutored the students in lighting, the chemistry of photography, the workings of lenses and shutters. But the strongest aspect of it all was that Bach organized the classes as if they were newspaper offices, with himself functioning like the city editor dishing out assignments.

Bach was not a teacher of salon photography. He intended to give youngsters practical skills and an ability to hold down jobs as photographers. "He urged us to anticipate things and to be aggressive and to keep shooting away," remembers Kauffman, "because he saw that kind of behavior as a prerequisite to mak-

16

ing it in the competitive business that is photography."

The students all owned secondhand Speed Graphics ("I can still smell the leather and glue that held mine together," says Mark) and Bach occasionally subsidized the youngster who couldn't afford to buy one.

In classes ahead of **Kauffman were Bob Landry, who became noted for his World War II photography** and the pinup of Rita Hayworth that launched her career; Johnny Florea who, like Landry, joined the staff of *Life* and was a war correspondent eventually to go into television; George Strock, whose controversial photographs of the bloated bodies of U.S. Marines lying half-buried on the beach of a South Pacific island brought home the war to America; and Art Rogers, who became chief photographer for the *Los Angeles Times*. Kauffman's contemporaries included John Dominis and Hank Walker, both of whom, like Kauffman, became *Life* staff photographers. And a few years behind Kauffman was John Zimmerman.

Like Kauffman, Zimmerman came from modest circumstances in Los Angeles, where he was born in 1927. His first camera was a Rolleicord, but once he started at Fremont with C. A. Bach he got a 3¼x4¼ Speed Graphic like everyone else. He was further en-

couraged by his father, who built a darkroom for him in their house. Zimmerman's father, a gaffer in a film studio, was a versatile craftsman who passed along much of his skill to his son. As a result, Zimmerman has been able to engineer and design what he wants in just about any camera.

Like Kauffman, Zimmerman also started out as a high school sports photographer. He and

A Marine DI chews out a raw recruit in Kauffman's memorable Life *essay.*

his fellow students also arranged to take pictures of the top entertainers at the local nightclubs and shows. Zimmerman photographed Nat King Cole, Bing Crosby and Woody Herman. He would then make up 11x14 prints in his lab and sell them to the celebrities for $1.50 apiece. To the youngster's surprise, the entertainers were happy to cooperate

in return for prints.

"But Bach emphasized sports photography because it offered so many approaches," explains Kauffman. "We could do portraits, still lifes, mood shots, play with the extremes of things like the seams and surfaces on balls and, of course, there was always the action."

Occasionally, when a heavy schedule stretched the manpower of the city's newspapers, the

neophytes were asked to handle minor events, including polo matches in Bel Air. "The polo teams were made up of the wealthiest people in town," says Kauffman. "But they welcomed us raggedy kids because they were hungry for publicity." The young photographers spent many hours driving around town in a battered old car equipped with a police radio. When word of an accident, a fire, a crime came over the air, the boys piled in with their Speed Graphics and rattled off to the scene. Bach had instructed them, however, in the rules of the game. If the kids found a newspaper's staff photographer present at the event, the youngsters would introduce themselves and then leave. Bach recognized that any sign that the Fremont students were competing with the older men would have disastrous consequences when they later went job-hunting.

The dream of young Mark Kauffman and most of his associates was to have a picture accepted by the new magazine *Life*. In 1939, when Kauffman was a 17-year-old senior and still had his curly hair, Eleanor Roosevelt came to Los Angeles. She agreed to be interviewed by the local student papers; each school was entitled to two people. Bach talked the principal at Fremont into sending a reporter and a photographer—Mark Kauffman. Equipped with his Speed Graphic and some old foil flashbulbs, Kauffman maneuvered to within six feet of Mrs. Roosevelt and took his pictures. Afterwards he developed them, and with Bach's blessing, sent his best prints to *Life*. Two weeks later came a telegram from the magazine telling the 17-year-old that his picture had been chosen for a cover. Kauffman would receive $50 for his cover portrait.

"I was an instant hero," says Kauffman, "someone to be talked about and pointed out. I got letters from the Board of Education telling me how proud they were. For a 17-year-old kid the role was very nice. The $50? It went to pay off debts I had run up for film, flashbulbs, and other items."

Immediately after high school, Kauffman went to work for a local photofinishing firm making enlargements, but was fired after two weeks on the job for rejecting everything but quality prints. Swallowing hard the businesslike notion that excellence was not a commercial goal, Kauffman next caught on as a darkroom assistant for Columbia Pictures. "I'd help with setups on stars like Rita Hayworth in the still studio, where I really learned something about lighting. And I kept bugging Johnny Florea, who worked for the *San Francisco Chronicle,* and Bob Landry, who was with International News Photos, to find an opening for me."

Bach nagged graduates of his programs to assist their juniors. "People like Landry didn't coach us as much as they served as models," says Kauffman. "They had made it. Landry was making $70 a week, which seemed like $500 a week today, and he drove around in a big Packard."

"What sticks in my mind most about meeting Landry," says Zimmerman, "was him showing us the engagement ring he'd bought for Deanna Durbin. But John de La Vega at the *Los Angeles Herald* and Art Rogers of the *Times,* both Fremont grads, got us assignments to do high school sports. The $5 a picture was nice, but I think we were all more impressed with having our stuff

printed than anything else. We were still short on imagination and a point of view. We simply roamed the sidelines waiting for something to happen in front of our cameras."

When Florea and Landry were hired by *Life* for its Los Angeles bureau, Kauffman pushed them harder. When another pair of hands was needed in the bureau's darkroom, Kauffman grabbed the offer, even though the salary was half of what he made at Columbia. He was hired on Friday afternoon, December 5, 1941. When he reported for work on Monday the United States was at war with Japan as a result of the attack on Pearl Harbor. All three *Life* staff photographers immediately left to cover the war. On his first day on the job as the lab technician, Kauffman discovered himself thrust out on the street, taking pictures for *Life*. "When I took the job I was a reasonably competent photographer. But I had figured it would take me a couple of years before there would be an opening. Suddenly there it

---

Zimmerman makes a stately church building seem to "fly" through downtown Detroit.

was. A hell of a break."

Even though he covered minor military matters, the Hollywood scene and did mug shots for *Time,* he piled up an impressive number of pages in Luce publications. He was, however, only 20 years old. With the war on, he succumbed to the call of the Marine Corps and enlisted in September, 1942. After boot camp Kauffman was transferred to the Fourth Marine Division as a combat reconnaissance photographer. He accompanied the Marines in landings at Kwajalein, Saipan, Tinian and Iwo Jima. After Iwo, as a staff sergeant, he was sent to officer candidate school in Quantico, Virginia. The war ended while he was there. Kauffman completed the course to be commissioned a second lieutenant and was put on inactive reserve. Out of this Marine background he drew the inspiration for a photo essay on the D.I. (drill instructor).

Like most young men in the war who matured by both experience and learning, Kauffman realized the effect of boot camp training upon the men, himself included, and determined to record the process in a photo essay. (One picture from

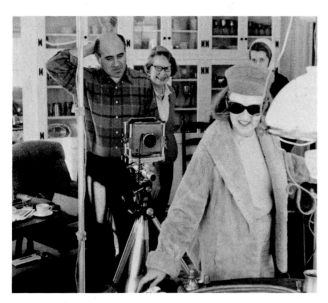

Kauffman did elaborate setups of great dinners for Life *and here works in the home of Bette Davis.*

the story appears on page 16.) W. Eugene Smith, the man who elevated the essay to its classical perfection, looks upon Kauffman's story as one of the great unacknowledged stories ever published by *Life*. "Individually," says Smith, "the pictures are not memorable. But collectively they form one of the great essays."

A powerful air of truth pervades the photographs. The Marines, although unhappy when the story was published, could not deny what Kauffman had shown so clearly. He demonstrated how the Marines couple physical conditioning with an all-out effort to strip the recruit of his individuality, turning him into a lethal automaton. It exemplifies Kauffman's focus on personal interaction between humans, which requires little of the vast armory of weapons that burden the photographer. Technical dross is pared to the minimum, permitting him to close in on human emotions and situations.

Kauffman's style becomes clearly illuminated through a contrast with that of John Zimmerman. For example, Zimmerman was assigned by *Life* to show the movement of the Mariner's Church in Detroit from one site to another, a three-block distance. The church traveled at a glacial speed on heavy log rollers in a trip that lasted four weeks.

The problem for Zimmerman was to convey in a photograph that the building (preceding page) was actually moving. He mounted a surveyor's transit on a Speed Graphic, affixed the whole apparatus to a movie tripod, and zeroed in on a single brick in the building. Then, during exposures of three to five minutes each, he panned the camera so that the crosshairs of the transit remained fixed on the brick while the church inched toward its new position. The church stayed in one spot on the film while its surroundings blurred, giving the effect of the church barreling through the city. What sets Zimmerman's approach apart from Kauffman's is not the time spent on a single photograph, but Zimmerman's use of the technology to create on film what even the naked eye could never have registered. Kauffman, on the other hand, works to freeze the actual moment as a way of emphasizing the situation.

Life sent Kauffman hopping to a variety of bureaus. While he was living in England he made a serious run at sports photography. During an assignment that took him to Helsinki, Kauffman met a lovely Finn named Anita Janssen; they shortly married and now have four daughters. Returning to London, Kauffman began to discover sport as the British knew it. He became something of a sport himself. John Dominis—Bach alumnus, *Life* colleague, and now the picture editor of *People*—recalls that when Kauffman returned to the States he sported an English accent and a dashing wardrobe. The affected accent is long gone, but the effect of English tailoring still survives. Kauffman is a natty dresser, an image that becomes him in his current position as Director of Photography for *Playboy*. While in England he also picked up a fondness for cigars and brandy from Winston

Mark Kauffman, currently Director of Photography for Playboy *magazine.*

Churchill while photographing the World War II leader for *Life*'s publication of the Churchill memoirs.

As *Life* continued to shift its people, Kauffman was brought back and assigned to the Washington bureau. "This is when I started to get it together," remarks Kauffman. "Until that time I had worked mainly with Rolleiflexes. I began to turn to Leicas and more and more 35mm work, because of the intimate involvement it afforded in stories like the D.I." The shift in focus gradually led to the University of Missouri's School of Journalism naming him a Photographer of the Year. Oddly enough, it

Silhouetting the surfcasters by backlighting emphasizes the solitary nature of the sport.

Panning is a chancey thing so when asked to shoot jai alai for Sports Illustrated *Kauffman tested the technique but protected himself by freezing the action as well.*

was the rather flaccid Eisenhower administration in Washington that forced Kauffman and others to devices that advanced the art of photojournalism. Never before had there been more picture opportunities or more intensive coverage of the political scene. The news magazines grew apace. Those were the halcyon years for *Life*. Television networks instituted nightly newscasts; presidential activities were broadcast live. All of this created a tremendous appetite for visual information, yet with all that journalistic talent present, the torpor of the Eisenhower years made it difficult to get strong pictures. Kauffman and his colleagues learned that with the longer, sharper lenses that were starting to come out of Japan, they could pull back from the pack and unobtrusively record facial expressions. Since the cameras

were not poking the pols in the face, the photographers were given some freedom to work at state occasions and newsmaking ceremonies. It was a throwback to that era of candid photojournalism typified by Dr. Eric Salomon working in Germany in the early 1930s.

During the fifties Kauffman and George Silk of *Life* began to experiment with a new rangefinder camera called the Foton, manufactured by Bell & Howell. It was the first genuine sequence camera. A Foton with its tight springwound motor could make up to six 35mm exposures in a second. Fotons were not only expensive but temperamental, and as a result they never made any dent in the photographic market.

"The chief limitation of

the Foton," says Kauffman, "was that the longest lens you could use with it was a 100mm. We adapted 200- and 300mm lenses to the Fotons and mounted a piece of tubing approximating the lens's perspective on top of the camera to serve as a finder. I tested it out at a baseball game and the damn thing worked beautifully."

Once upon a time photographers had actually been permitted to work on the baseball field, but that plan was scotched by enthusiastic cameramen like Hy Peskin. A celebrated sports photographer of the day, Peskin was working a close game between the Giants and the Dodgers from a spot behind first base one day when he saw a ball hit into right field. He realized that there would be a close play at third. With the volatile Leo Durocher coaching at third, Peskin just knew there would be a scene. As the right-fielder chased down the ball, Peskin took the shortest route to the site of action—a straight line right across the diamond—thereby managing

to arrive at third simultaneously with the ball and
runner. Peskin got his
pictures, but such antics
by such photographers
later caused all photog-
raphers to be barred ac-
cess to the playing areas
during the game.

But the Cleveland dia-
mond was still an open
field for Kauffman when
he toted his jury-rigged
Foton to the game. His
work there earned a
two-page spread in

Life, an unprecedented
amount of space for the
magazine to give such a
topic. Moreover, other
photographers caught a
glimmer of the new pos-
sibilities in sports pho-
tography and soon
began to experiment.
Kauffman's device was
far more portable than
the cumbersome tripod-
mounted 4x5 Graflex
cameras with 30- to 40-
inch lenses that were
then the standard. Be-

cause of their size they
had to be operated from
high up in the photog-
raphers' gallery. Sports
photography took on a
new perspective when
Kauffman walked onto
the field with his cam-
eras. In addition, the
motor mechanism practi-
cally guaranteed a pic-
ture of the moment of
peak action.

"I was tired of the Big
Berthas that looked
down on the athletes as

Funny toppers to keep the troops cool At the last practice before the game coaches invent ways to ease the week-long tension with games and jokes. At Marina Ferry the icebreaker is hats. Sterling players show up wearing the oddest-looking headgear they can find. Here, Fullback Dave Joseph and Tackle Curt Dagler show off some unlikely chapeaux. Their tough, confident look has earned team's nicknames like "The Mafia" and "The Untouchables." Though most of the good players are so bulking as the pair below, there are dozens of toothpicks who weigh 45 pounds wringing wet but still obey the big boys down to their size.

Sport has always been a writer's game. It makes good copy. And because writers become editors of magazines, photographers get short shrift. The game-winning touchdown is enough from them. Thus, the conceptualization of sports photography came to be single pictures. Only the writer was allowed to flesh out his portrait with human details.

Photographers' most vivid form of communication—picture essay—was pioneered by Life in this country in the late thirties. Surprisingly, it took twenty years before sport was considered an apt subject for it. Mark Kauffman was a pioneer of the sports essay. One of the finest evocations of the gritty spirit of football was made by him when he turned his attention to a rude mill town where high school football is the only diversion and the only escape.

if they were toy soldiers,"
says Kauffman. "There's
a great Walter Mitty
character in spectators
at a sports event. I
wanted to bring the
viewer into the action,
give him an intimacy
with the body contact,
the speed, the tension
on the field. The Foton
helped me make sure I
caught the split second,
and a long lens allowed
me to put the focus
where I wanted it, on the
action, as experienced
by the players them-
selves."

In approaching even
so sedate a sport as
fishing, Kauffman tried
for a new look to replace
the standard shot of an
angler holding a string of
very dead specimens. He
set out to evoke the solitary satisfaction of the
activity (page 19). "A
surf caster gets out on
the beach when it's still
in the dark of morning.
There's a feeling of qui-
etude, broken only by
water lapping the beach,
and the whine of line
cast out to sea. You're
alone until the sun rises,
a fantastic light spreads
over the horizon and
gradually you turn to see
that there are other surf
casters—companions in
solitude—scattered
about."

That sensitivity to the
nuances of the human
equation stood Kauffman
in good stead when he
turned his talents to the
sports essay. With writer
Jack McDermott, Mark
traveled to Martin's
Ferry, Ohio, the very bed-
rock of football in this
country. Located just
over the line from the
West Virginia coal mining
territory, the region has
turned out an astonish-
ing number of profes-
sional athletes. "For the
kids there," says Kauff-
man, "football was one
of the few ways to es-
cape the mines and
the desolation. Even if
you weren't good

'You ain't dead yet
by a long shot'

"We come off the field two ways," says a Valley play
we're ordered or we're carried." To bind their scarred kn
bruised legs, they wear hand pads, knee braces or whe

72

Rocky Cradle
of Football

Photographed for LIFE by MARK KAUFFMAN

CONTINUED   70A

team trainer can devise to keep them in the game.
er will be encouraged to straighten up by his team-
of "What's your name? Candy?" If he stumbles to

the sidelines the coach will give him even less sympathy. "Where
does it hurt?" asks the coach. "Your knee? Why hell, son, that's
four feet away from your heart. You ain't dead yet by a long shot."

CONTINUED   73

enough to play pro ball, you might still qualify for a scholarship at some college and earn a ticket to somewhere else. For the people who stayed in Martin's Ferry, high school football was a way of life, one of the few pursuits in that drab locale that enabled them to escape the struggle to survive.''

A double-truck picture of the game played against a tatty backdrop of gray frame houses and the begrimed school set the scene. The rickety stands, the gathering of the blue-collar spectators, the absence of sky and the foreshortening that brings the buildings oppressively tight, all add up to convey a mood of gloom. Kauffman then personalized Martin's Ferry with portraits: a boy with a hat that belongs back in the summer of '42, another of a youth with flat features and solid physique carved by the terrain. And zooming in from afar with a telephoto lens, he makes the coach the epitome of a football field marshal.

The photographer rammed home the primeval quality of the place with a sharp-eyed attention to details: the fingers thrust into the mud, the flimsy protection over the knuckles, the open wound on the arm, the patched shoes, the newly-applied bandage. In such homely trifles are the makings of great essays. It didn't require impressive credentials, or

a planeload of professional athletes. It was found on a small town high school lot by a mindful photographer.

Dirt, poverty **of the mind and body, as well as the violence of life,** have been stock subjects for many photojournalists. Indeed, certain photographers have been able to record only the ugly and the bizarre. Kauffman, however, also has the capacity to appreciate and photograph the beauty of moments well removed from the ruck of mere subsistence. More so than any other ambiance, the British scene taught him that a sports photograph need not only consist of fury and quest. The magnificent greens of the damp, tempered climate and the upper-class devotion to the preservation of that delightful institution known as cricket (at left) were united by Kauffman in a graceful portrait of another kind of sport. Here, Kauffman capitalized on a framing of leafy green for the white-garbed cricketers. The technique is reminiscent of his composition of a solitary punter framed by spring foliage (page 1). The photographer responded to the environment, the atmosphere with its pleasant air of civility, and included it in his interpretation of the story.
Among Kauffman's fin-

Using the existing foliage as a frame Kauffman made a statement about the gentlemanly game of cricket.

Getting up close with a wide-angle lens Kauffman was able to capture all the thundering intensity of the steeplechase.

26

est investigations of England was his essay on the special flavor of their horseracing. The British version differs markedly from the U.S. sport, for reasons that go well beyond the practice of running their horses in the opposite direction to the Americans'. In the United States racing is basically a money game; the tracks, the events and the parimutuel betting are all styled to increase the wagering take. The British way retains some of the ancient rural roots. Workouts, instead of being restricted to a sterile track atmosphere, often send animals over the glorious green of the countryside. The steeplechase, which still thrives in England, traces its antecedents to a time when the horse was a partner in the hunt. The betting is still handled by bookies

rather than a computer. The sport has also managed to retain its hold on the landed and the elegant, yet continues to attract the working class and the young.

To do his essay on British racing, Kauffman positioned himself, and in some instances installed a remote-controlled camera, in strategic spots near the jumps of the steeplechases. The side view of horses soaring over a hedge (preceding page) was made with a hand-held Nikon equipped with a 35mm wide-angle lens. For the head-on photographs of the charging horses rising at a jump (pages 30–31) he planted a motor drive with a remote control switch at the base of the hedge. It was one of the first times that the viewer was placed where nobody, not even a photographer, had ever been before.

"Patience and the right to take your time are most valuable in an essay," Kauffman says. "One aim of mine was to draw a contrast between the violent action of the actual races and the training periods (this page and next). The picture of the horses galloping over

the fields was done in the west of England with a 135mm lens on a Leica. I'm only sorry that it's impossible to also get across the difference in the sounds. When the horses are training in the morning, they pant gently. You can hear dewdrops falling from the foliage. At the races, the ear is dominated by the roaring crowd and the pounding hooves." Kauffman of course did not scant the human element; after the race a victorious jockey hauling his tack proudly sports his badge of mud.

Among the advantages of magazine living were the endless expense-account meals in all corners of the globe. Kauffman and Zimmerman developed their instincts for good food and fine wines and might have been the original galloping gourmets. In the later years of *Life* Kauffman was shooting many of the Great Dinner series in 8x10 color. Eventually he opened up a commercial studio with complete kitchen facilities that became a gathering spot for all-night poker parties, with Kauffman whipping up exotic dishes in the kitchen and wiping out the opposition at the card table. "When Kauffman and Zimmerman were both in town," recalls a former *Life* editor, "there was a great deal of culinary one-upsmanship. Just going to a lunch counter in the basement of the *Time-Life* building with those guys was a fascinating show."

By nature a curious man, Kauffman continually strives to add to his fund of information, particularly anything he expects to photograph. Perhaps the best example of his attitude appeared in the first issue of *Sports Illustrated*. The lead story covered the

Kauffman casts a reportorial eye on horse racing in England with his pictures of the stable activity, a begrimed jockey and early morning workouts over open fields. As befitting the simple elegance of the sport he used his standard lens.

drove by Landy into the home stretch, Kauffman was on the spot to record the climax. Some people chalk up Kauffman's picture to a lucky guess. But Branch Rickey, the patriarch of professional baseball, once remarked, ''Luck is the residue of design.'' At Vancouver, Kauffman made Rickey's maxim a verity.

In a completely different vein, Kauffman showed how to turn a still life into a thoughtful expression of movement and aerodynamics. The Museum of Modern Art in New York once held an exhibition of sports-equipment design, and Kauffman decided to group those materials that held some common aspects: protective masks, various balls that contrasted in size, shape

British Empire Games in Vancouver, where the world's first sub-four-minute milers, Briton Roger Bannister and Australian John Landy, were to compete. When Kauffman drew the assignment to cover the race, he huddled with writer Paul O'Neill. From him, Kauffman learned the tactics that the runners were expected to follow. Landy was a front-runner, while Bannister preferred to make his move late in the race. Adding up the information, Kauffman paced off a certain distance from the finish line where, if all went according to plan, Bannister could be expected to challenge Landy for the lead.

While Kauffman stationed himself at this point, the other photographers all gathered at

the finish line for the traditional picture. The race followed the book perfectly. At the precise moment that Bannister

A remote-controlled motor drive catches this cascade of charging horseflesh.

31

and texture and, as on pages 6–7, two vehicles designed for special racing. The formula race car and the harness sulky share a desire to eliminate wind resistance, and the parallelism of the right-hand side of the photograph captures this aspect of design. The concentric wheels provide another touchstone of commonality. The photographer has arranged for the car's oblong shape to tug against the sulky's basically circular one. Many of Kauffman's compositions stand on a basic premise of art and philosophy, the introduction of tension through contrasting forces. His treatment of car and sulky, while distinguishing the two shapes, encapsulates the peculiar aerodynamic qualities of each.

For all his success at stopping action or at creating a sense of it in a still life. Kauffman is well aware that the speed of the shutters, films and lenses can conspire to rob sports events of some drama. The dilemma is to record movement without making it seem inactive. Kauffman chose

Panning shows the flow of motion but should be considered an experiment when working under pressure. This baton pass at the Millrose Games is a Sports Illustrated *classic but was attempted only because another staffer was present to shoot it normally allowing Kauffman the license to experiment.*

the technique of panning as one way to deal with the problem.

''Panning is,'' says Kauffman, ''something like shooting in the dark. One reason to pan is obviously for the effect of presenting a flowing action. But the difficulty is that it is practically impossible to predict the final result. Background

colors will move and blend together, giving shades and tones and creating hues which you cannot, in most cases, forecast. It's such a chancy thing that many photographers can't afford to risk it because the editor counts on having at least one tacksharp photo of the principals in the event.

Therefore they never gamble with a pan on an important news event. When on assignment, you always go for the money—get the picture that they need first—then, if you have time, experiment with pans.'' Nevertheless, at the Millrose Games in Madison Square Garden, Kauffman was willing to risk a pan on the path of a baton in the relay races (below).

The choice of lens is vital to the success of the panning technique. If given an opportunity to choose, Kauffman opts for the longest lens possible. The farther the camera is away from the arc being transcribed by the front of the lens, the slower the photographer can pan and the more control he has. Also to be considered is the speed of the telephoto lens in relationship to the existing light. The field of view should be wide enough to accommodate the anticipated composition. And last, the section of the field to be covered by the arc—

especially the foreground—should be free of obstructions such as posts, signs and wandering spectators.

A wide-angle lens creates a different effect but requires considerable dexterity. The photographer must be extremely close to the action to get an effective image size, yet that causes the subject to move through the viewfinder at blinding speed. Because of the lens's great depth of field, the streaked pattern is sharp and pronounced. The wide-angle lens's natural distortion causes the streaks to move in an arc. The technique is especially effective in covering auto racing. The cars appear to bend on their axis. The tires assume an oval shape. The entire machine seems to be straining to get around a corner.

"The art of panning is to move the camera in the same direction as the flow of the action," explains Kauffman. "You must start to track well before you actually trip the shutter in order to get a flow that harmonizes the movement of camera and subject. I favor shutter speeds of 1/15 to 1/8 second.

You should shoot somewhere in the middle of the panning motion and remember to continue to swing the camera in a follow-through motion even after you have taken the picture. That prevents a jerking stop which screws it up. If you use a motor drive, you should begin your shooting even earlier. Most cameras have in their viewfinders a hatching or centerpoint. I liken this to a gunsight and keep my game right in the crosshairs all the time. At the midpoint of my arc I squeeze off the shot and continue the motion even after the mirror returns the view."

Panning became simplified with the development of the motor drive. Prior to this advance in technology, the need to re-cock the shutter interrupted the smooth swing of the camera. The motorized camera also reduced the risk of missing a vital piece of action. One of the attractions of panning, so far as Kauffman is concerned, is its change of pace, the fun and relief from the hard-edge image produced by strobe-lit action, or fast shutter speeds. Even though he recognizes that panning can mean flirtation with disaster, Kauffman had enough confidence in his ability to control the picture at such a critical event as the women's 100-meter dash in the Rome Olympics. "When Wilma Rudolph hit the finish line," says Kauffman, "I wanted a clean background to make her stand out. I always re-

Gold medalist Wilma Rudolph luckily struck a classic pose at the finish but Kauffman's picture wouldn't have been nearly as effective without his sharp-eyed attention to the details of having a clear background.

search the background of my photographs. It is extremely important, and something that I learned from studying the work of Henri Cartier-Bresson. From my original position in the photographer's gallery I noticed some hurdles resting in the infield intruding into the composition. I left my colleagues huddled at the finish line and moved down the gallery until the hurdles were out of my viewfinder.''

The mark of the professional is that constant scrutiny for fine detail. Not content with merely capturing the peak action, Kauffman arranges to have the best possible backdrop flatter his composition. But assume that there had been a gallery of spectators all along the infield from which there was no escape. Kauffman would have used backlighting. Maintaining the same angle to the finish line, Kauffman would have crossed the track and assumed a position in the opposite stands facing the sun. If it was too low and directly in his lens he would seek distance and elevation. Exposing for the shadow necessitates a wide aperture, which reduces depth of field and turns the offending background into a muted, out-of-focus pattern. Admittedly, it would have been a harsher, more contrasty picture, but less of a problem than a bad background.

''Rudolph was a slight pan, done at a high speed, 1/25 at f/16,'' says Kauffman. ''I took the extra f/stop with the lens to give her a little depth of field. She was fast, and I didn't want her to move out of my focus. I had prefocused on her lane, but had been following her with the camera since she started the race. Luckily we all arrived at the

The longer the lens the easier it is to follow fast action. For sprinters the medium length telephoto lenses are ideal.

same point at the same time. What really made the picture was her position as she came to the tape. That's something you can never predict.''

The baton-passing photo on pages 32–33, the Wilma Rudolph finish and the sprinters (above) indicate how much variety Kauffman could generate for a single event using one technique. While Kauffman was in Vancouver for the Empire Games, he considered the soothing rhythm of the cycle races a counterpart to the explosive race between Bannister and Landy. On the picture he made from overhead onto the track (next

page) Kauffman says, ''I got a sense of tranquillity during the quiet moment of the bike races, and panned to give it that sense of moment.''

Apart from the photographer's flawless technique, the smoothness of the pan is attributable to the constant speed maintained by the bicycles. Human locomotion is a lot less efficient, as the body decelerates for an instant every time the foot hits the ground. The consistency of the forward motion of a wheeled vehicle makes for a sharp picture. Had Kauffman been photographing a motorcycle sprint, or a stock car race where he wanted to convey the rough, raucous nature of the sport, he would have panned slower or faster than the vehicle, or perhaps added some vertical movement to his arc to take the even edge off the subjects.

To come up with a strong image from ringside during the momentous heavyweight title bout demands no extraordinary ability. The incident itself usually packs enough wallop to carry even a routine pic-

ture. But to be shunted away from the site of action and still capture the drama in an exquisite composition tests the merit of any photographer. In the fifties, *Sports Illustrated* campaigned vigorously against the control of boxing by racketeers. The magazine had suggested that some executives of Madison Square Garden had demonstrated an unhealthy affinity for members of the underworld. When the Garden promoted a fight between heavyweight champion Rocky Marciano and challenger Archie Moore, the request by *Sports Illustrated* for photographers' positions at ringside was rejected. There was no court of higher appeal from the decision.

The magazine had to buy some tickets for the fight, and Kauffman, anxious to see the match, received one. In hopes that he might be able to at least get something on the spectators, he brought along a camera. His seat was in the fourteenth row. A startlingly attractive woman was sitting next to him. Once the fight began, the lady complained that she couldn't see what was happening, so Kauffman handed her his camera with a 200mm lens on it. But by the third round Marciano began to belt Moore unmercifully, and Kauffman decided to retrieve it. Moore started to go down, the crowd erupted. Some stood on chairs. Kauffman jumped up on his. While the woman held his legs, he shot a dozen frames. In that small take were two classics—but even one would have been all that was necessary. Taken at 1/125 at f/5.6, the first showed Moore collapsing while he grabbed for support at the ropes. The second picture, and the one eventually used

The smooth symmetry of the cyclists is enhanced by panning and Kauffman's position capitalized on their shadows to modify his composition.

in the magazine (next page) is a classic tableau of a fight's end. The existing light of the murky arena adds a dramatic context that would have been burned away had Kauffman used strobes. The champion has returned to his corner stool. The exultant crowd is still on its feet, framing part of the picture. Aides are clambering through the ropes. And a vanquished, still dazed Archie Moore half walks, half crawls over to congratulate Marciano.

"I doubt very much if I could have made as good a picture if I had been in the first row," says Kauffman. "I needed the distance to get all of the elements: two fighters, referee, fans, background.

"It also proves my point," insists Kauffman. "The eye is what's most important. The picture shows that having press seats at ringside or on the field isn't always necessary and sometimes isn't even best. A fan who has some expertise with a camera with a long lens, usually a 135mm or longer, can with some planning not only see the event but get some damn good pictures. Being a little out of the center of the scene provides angles for unusual photographs. Technique is only a tool. You can make the same

A beaten Archie Moore and Rocky Marciano in one of boxing's most emotional moments. Kauffman captured it from his spectator seat in the 14th row.

kind of pictures if you're working at a high school gym or in a small nightclub, or are working out of a fairly good seat at a stadium." The only difference is that the amateur probably can't count on having a beautiful woman—who turned out to be Lauren Bacall—hold him steady on the chair.

John Zimmerman: Advancing Camera Technology

Early in the 1950s, Coles Phinizy, a correspondent for *Life* working out of the Atlanta bureau, received an assignment to cover a story with a new freelance photographer named John G. Zimmerman. They were to meet at the site of the event. "How will I know which photographer is Zimmerman?" asked Phinizy.

"Just look for the guy who is screwing his equipment back together," was the answer. Recalls Phinizy, "Sure enough, when I got there I saw this photographer on a ladder. As I approached him, the camera he was putting back together fell apart. It was Zimmerman."

Whether or not the anecdote is apocryphal, John Zimmerman is associated with the technology of the camera. In

almost a lifelong fascination with machinery while making pictures for *Sports Illustrated, Life, Saturday Evening Post,* commercial work, even movies, Zimmerman has consistently innovated and explored the range of cameras.

His early training with C. A. Bach convinced him that he wanted to be a photographer, but he had a slow start. Zimmerman spent an uneventful period in the Navy after high school graduation, and took odd jobs working for International News and the *Life* Los Angeles bureau. When a job opened up as a *Life* darkroom man in Washington, the young man went east. Later, on his first assignment as a *Time* staff photographer, he was leaving the White House and heard shots near Blair House, where President Harry Truman was then living while repairs were being made on the White House. Just then Puerto Rican nationalists laid siege to the building and Zimmerman got some of the first photos of the assault. But, surprisingly for a Bach graduate, he lacked the requisite hustle of a newsman. He never tried to use these pictures as leverage to get more assignments from *Life.* Zimmerman wanted to create pictures, and wasn't content with merely recording the action.

Yet that extraordinary luck would follow him and, as before, he would have the remarkable prescience and quick reflexes to capture the action, even if it wasn't completely of his own choosing. He was doing an ad for an agency that was to show the number of different military planes that used General Electric engines. The idea was to show them

John G. Zimmerman

in flight all flying in formation. One of the aircraft was the highly experimental XB-70. Zimmerman actually received the assignment because he was one of the few photographers accredited to fly in military jets.

"Naturally, when it came time to take the pictures of a government airplane," Zimmerman remembers, "we couldn't get the use of a military aircraft. So we managed to borrow Frank Sinatra's Lear Jet."

The Lear was slower than the other planes, so Zimmerman had the military pilots orbit around the photo ship. He had his cameras ready for each occasion that they swept by. He had finished the still work and a film crew was waiting for the formation to make another pass when suddenly his pilot yelled, "Take a picture! Take a

picture!" Another jet had clipped the tail of the XB-70. "Maybe he was caught in the vortex off the wings of the bigger plane," says Zimmerman. "Nobody will ever know. But a big orange fireball roared by us. The first ship broke up and the XB-70 spun wildly around and started down. I kept taking pictures, using motor-driven Nikons with both 35- and 50mm lenses, and followed the XB-70 down until it crashed on the desert floor." When he landed the Air Force confiscated Zimmerman's film. Afterwards, they released some of the material for *Life* (at right) and picture editor Dick Pollard paid Zimmerman space rates even though the photos had come from the Air Force as a handout. The agency also paid Zimmerman's full $6,000 fee.

Much more in the Zimmerman style was his recreation of the glamour of open cockpit flying. Zimmerman in this instance relied heavily upon remote control cameras and the daring aerial wizardry of pilots Frank Tallman and Paul Mantz, owners of a flying museum in Orange County, California. "Tallman dug up some old flying togs, trimmed with a flamboyant scarf that trailed out of the cockpit, and then flew some of the damndest machines," Zimmerman recalls. "One was an early Bleriot that was steered by pulling on cables that warped the wings. He headed out over the Pacific in the thing."

Tallman put on dogfights with rickety contraptions—a Fokker D-7 and a Spad—that climbed, dived, looped and spun in mock duels for the benefit of a one-man audience and his cameras. Much of the time Zimmerman flew in an LT-1, a strafing aircraft whose machine gun and canopy had been removed so that Zimmerman could hang out with his cameras for an unobstructed view. He was held in by two straps while the slipstream tore at his body, whipped his hair and tried to strip away his cameras. "The best I can say for that old goose of a plane was 'that it was one of the few times I didn't get airsick," says Zimmerman. For all the time he's spent bobbing on boats or circling in small planes and helicopters, Zimmerman is uncommonly prone to airsickness.

"I used to be able to fill two or three bags, easily," he says. "Happily I'm getting over it. Taking those pills only makes me drowsy. Looking through a viewfinder helps, but when the horizon becomes disoriented and your head is down loading film, while the pilot is in tight maneuvers, it can become quite unpleasant. But if you're careful and not hurried you can do just about anything. I'm not really fascinated by flying so much as by the extraordinary images it affords."

To show the antique airplane in its steep bank (next page) Zimmerman put his trust in Tallman both as a pilot and a cameraman. They mounted a 250-exposure-back Nikon on the fuselage with the wire to the remote switch running down the joy stick. It was equipped with a 28mm lens set at f/16 and 1/15 second to give a blur that would transmit the feeling of a spin. All the stunts were worked out on the ground before Tallman took off. But the amount of light and its direction were uncontrollable. Sometimes Tallman headed directly into the sun; on other maneuvers he would fly out of it. In most aerial photography the pilots are under rigid instructions to fly in such a relationship to the sun as to not vary the exposure. "I wanted him to do everything and not worry about exposure," says Zimmerman. "I was planning on some happy accidents to occur. With a wide-angle lens I knew that even if the sun was in the picture there wouldn't be enough flare to ruin it."

Actually the pilot's original instruction for the picture was to illustrate a roll. The viewer identifies it as such by the clear vortex in the center of the whirling color. Had the pilot executed a perfect maneuver the open tunnel would be on line with the midpoint of the aircraft from nose to tail to ground, and would be totally obscured by its stabilizers at the rear of the aircraft. In fact, the pilot executed a slipping roll that placed the eye off-center and in the full view of the camera—another happy accident. On page 44 Zimmerman wanted the entire ground to appear sharp. He used the same camera setup, but this time increased the shutter speed to 1/500 second. Although the camera had not been moved, the simple changing of the shutter speed created pictures of entirely different feeling. The slower shutter creates the dizzying background that shows the aircraft's relationship to the sky. The faster shutter fixes the

Last Seconds of the Doomed Superjet XB-70

A cry of 'Midair!'—distress call for collision

A maelstrom of muted color conveys the sensation of a spin in Zimmerman's Saturday Evening Post story on the glories of open cockpit flying. It was accomplished by a remote-controlled camera set at a slow shutter speed.

sharp background that shows the aircraft's relationship to the earth.

The antique airplanes were part of a memorable essay that Zimmerman did for the *Saturday Evening Post.* Just when his career was blooming at *Life,* he jumped to *Sports Illustrated* and then, just as he found his niche there, he took a staff position with the *Post.* "John is a very impressionable guy," says a friend. "He always has his ear to the ground in this business. He listens to what photographers and editors are saying, and reacts accordingly. Throughout his career he has made abrupt moves from some very secure and very lucrative positions that, at the time, seemed ill-advised, but he always manages to improve his lot. The changes are not motivated by money so much as a way of widening his knowledge of the craft."

Just after moving to New York he was so unknowing as to book a flight from his home base to Philadelphia, only 83 miles away. In the brief trip between the two cities he met a dark-haired stewardess named Dolores Miter. In 1958 TWA lost her to marriage and they now have three children, two boys 16 and 14, and a daughter 12. The union hardly slowed him down. Dolores Zimmer-

Changing the shutter speed to freeze the aircraft's position in the sky created a totally different feeling.

man says of those days, "He was on the road so much that I was forced to become a partner in the business so I could get to see him. When he returned to freelancing I eventually assumed the whole financial operation."

Zimmerman is on assignment 250 days in a typical year. In 1972 they moved to Los Angeles as John began to do more commercial work, using his technical expertise to illustrate complex concepts for advertising clients and his impeccable lighting approaches to become a much sought-after architectural photographer. They live in a gracious colonial house that they have remodeled to include two studios—one for the husband-photographer and another for the artist-wife. As keeper of the books, Dolores

despairs at times of her husband's exacting standards for his work. "He won a contract in 1974 to do the pictures for MGM's new hotel in Las Vegas and the money looked very good until John became so determined to make everything of the highest caliber that the financial rewards shrank. We often wind up subsidizing the client."

John Frook, former *Life* West Coast bureau chief, now a business associate of Zimmerman's, was with him on the recent MGM assignment. "He cares desperately about his craftsmanship," says Frook. "In an era of declining professionalism, there are too many photographers working who couldn't carry the camera bags of someone like Zimmerman. Alas, they are out there, and they

taint the good ones. Clients do appreciate quality. They are flabbergasted when someone takes the time to get the green out of fluorescent and balance it with daylight. It's a matter of course with Zimmerman. He's a worldbeater who loves his work."

Zimmerman's pace is legend. He worked 11 days straight inside the hotel without ever taking a break for so much as a set of tennis, in which, a recent victim claims, "he has the instincts of a barracuda." In one sprint against deadline he shot for 30 straight hours before his two young assistants quit in exhaustion. Zimmerman continued on and finished the job by himself the next day.

Such a shooting day begins on a deceptively graceful note, Frook reports. "Zimmerman has an anachronistic gentlemanly quality that is delightful. He invites you to his room for an ample catered breakfast. He goes over the day's shooting schedule down to the minutest detail, all the while sitting there with the ever-present pipe, the half-frame spectacles sliding down his nose, and wrapped up in his robe and slippers. You comment on the robe and slippers, and he proudly shows you another set he has brought along. Who the hell takes a dressing robe to Las Vegas—and who has two of them! Every contingency is planned for!"

When he was a staff photographer for *Sports Illustrated* Zimmerman did a story on life in front of the hockey net. If you probe the psyche of sports photographers you'll find a deep resentment of authority—in their cases it's a resentment of the owners, managers, ushers and

other photographers who say to them "it can't be done." For Zimmerman the challenge to his technical expertise and creative energies was too much when he got the idea to photograph the epicenter of the game's most furious action.

Zimmerman **wanted to put two of his cameras inside the corners of the goal-tender's cage** at the New York Ranger hockey games. There was resistance at first, but he kept badgering the team's management. The photographer would operate the cameras from the first row behind the net and fire remotely the one with the best view of the action unobscured by the goalie. "Everybody passed the buck on whether or not we could try it. Finally we reached the Rangers' general manager who said that he wasn't able to find anything in the rule book that said we couldn't."

Zimmerman hauled his electronic flash equipment into the Garden and hung four of the Sunlight series of Ascors from the mezzanine rows in each corner of the rink. The Garden ceiling was too high to be of any use as a place to hang lights, so he had to put them low, within

The remote control camera puts the viewer where no-body—even a photographer—has ever been before.

camera range. Luckily he was using a wide-angle lens throughout, so any flare would not dominate the picture. The Garden agreed to lay the remote wires under the ice in back of the goal but the whole project nearly aborted when the employee responsible for burying the wire forgot his assignment. An hour before game time a technician hurriedly chopped a rut in the ice, placed the wire in the trench and then poured water over it. By game time the new ice had formed over the wire lead. During the game, however, Zimmerman noticed to his horror that the ice covering the wire had been shaved away by the skaters. A New York Ranger in hot pursuit of the puck stumbled as he skated over the exposed lead. He turned to seek the cause, but his concern for the game distracted him from finding it. Between periods repairs were made and it was safely buried again. The pictures (one is below) earned seven pages in *Sports Illustrated.*

Some years later *Life* invited Zimmerman to focus on Bobby Orr, the superstar of the Boston Bruins. Short of getting on the ice with Orr during a game—that definitely couldn't be done—the best way of showing Orr's aggressive play was from the goalie's viewpoint. Again, the John Zimmerman show went on the road. But as a defenseman Orr doesn't make that many shots on goal. The assignment was one long, exasperating wait. Zimmerman stalked Orr for six games before he finally got the picture on the next page. And again, disaster nibbled at the edges. One member of

Although the technique is the same as before, different lighting, different players—especially the formidable Bobby Orr—create another kind of picture. "The best picture has yet to be made," Zimmerman suggests.

47

Plate glass partially smeared with Vaseline and mounted away from the lens gives this controlled blur of rushing color.

the visiting team practiced his slap shot by aiming at the camera so neatly tucked into the back of the net. The cap proved inadequate protection against a hard rubber puck traveling 100 mph that, in one swift single hit, shattered the lens.

Although it will never be noted in any of the records of the National Hockey League, during his six days with Bobby Orr Zimmerman scored a goal against the Bruins. White tape had made the cameras blend into the background of the boards but there was no camouflage for the lenses themselves. Somebody took a shot during a game and the puck bounced off a goalpost and back into play. But the official skating by glimpsed a round black object in the net (the lens) and sig-

naled a goal. The Bruins screamed and protested but the goal stood. "I was not very popular since it cost them the game, 2–1," says Zimmerman. "I wasn't forgiven until after they won the Stanley Cup."

To bring readers up close to basketball, Zimmerman again put remote-controlled cameras on the target, this time behind the glass backboards. He used black tape to camouflage the equipment, mounted on the backboard supports. For Kareem Abdul Jabbar (at right), Zimmerman used a battery-operated Hasselblad—the only time he's ever used that camera. Mounting a remote camera with a fixed focus requires some research on the subject's playing style. As a rookie—then known as Lew Alcindor—Jabbar was feared for his fadeaway hook shot. Observation showed that he favored the left side from close to the board, so that was where Zimmerman aimed and focused.

The fugue of color rising to the basketball backboard (above) grew out of an old-fashioned trick of shooting through a large 11x14 pane of glass that was placed in front of

the camera and smeared with Vaseline. The advantage over a commercially-bought soft-focus filter or one handmade out of a skylight filter is that the photographer gets soft swirling colors while retaining some control. He can determine which area to keep clear, or whether to blur the edges, the top or the bottom half of the frame. By applying the Vaseline in patterns—circles, streaks, squiggles—he can create different effects. The lighting is carefully designed to fall only on the players so as to create a deep black canvas, uninterrupted by confusing elements like spectators, upon which Zimmerman paints the impressionistic colors. "Sure it could be done in the darkroom afterwards with less margin for error," Zimmerman admits. "But that takes the excitement out of it for me. You get better color quality if it is done on the original film. And there's always room for an accident in which the forms and colors come together with an image that goes beyond anything you could plan or execute in the darkroom."

He attributes his photograph of Wilt Chamberlain's dunk shot (pages 50–51) to patience:

Researching Jabbar's favorite shot, Zimmerman then prefocused his remote camera mounted on the backboard and waited. It took three games before Jabbar came to him with the picture Zimmerman wanted.

Wilt Chamberlain stuffs one in full view of Zimmerman's remote shooting through the clear glass backboard.

54

Whether he is covering a race or a resort Zimmerman prepares by skiing all the courses at least twice (in the morning light and at dusk) before he photographs so as to find the best possible vantage points.

52

High above Lake Okanagan, Art Furrer makes one turn through the morning snow (left), and (by Bernhard Russi of Switzerland, Olympic downhill champion, shown at far right). Matt Oehlert, who donned the wild-barred hat in the mountains.

"You knew he'd be up there sooner or later." A Nikon with a 28mm lens supplied the sense of giantism that made Chamberlain such a gate draw for the National Basketball Association.

Growing up near the Southern California film community, Zimmerman could easily mistake snow for the cornstarch that they used on the lots. Actually he had not skied much before *Sports Illustrated* assigned him his first ski story, but with that he became an addict, eventually infecting his entire family with his enthusiasm. When it was blowing or snowing and conditions were too foul for shooting, most photographers would head for the bar. But Zimmerman would be out on the slopes practicing. His pictures of skiing have done almost as much as stretch pants to make the sport attractive. It became something of a joke among the photographers who showed up for the various winter games. While others nursed their hot toddies and glüg hangovers on frigid mornings, Zimmerman rose with the sun to ski the areas in search of clues that would enable him to anticipate a picture. "It's a grind," Zimmerman says. "Your

Photographing powder skiing requires precision. Once a skier passes through, the location has been marred. Zimmerman marks his spot by throwing a snowball to it, focusing and then instructs his skier to hit the spot.

equipment feels like it weighs a ton as you try to ski and see everything at least twice. You end up exhausted and sweaty, but it's a great way to fitness and the only way to good pictures, I'm convinced."

It was through such early morning treks that Zimmerman discovered a breathtaking vantage point at Sapporo, Japan, the Disney-like setting for the 1972 Winter Olympics (page 53, top).

Competitive skiing, however, limits creative possibilities. Zimmerman has been far better able to evoke the ecstasy of the average skier, the crisp, cold loveliness of the sport, when his only mission has been to introduce a way of skiing or a place to ski, such as the Bugaboo area in Canada (page 53 bottom).

"Like in most outdoor photography," Zimmerman advises, "midday is the worst possible time to shoot. In the high country the sun illuminates the snow so brightly that all detail is lost. The mountains are normally all washed out, without the dramatic shadows that produce shape and form. It is best to work either early in the day or late, to-

wards dusk, when the contrast is not so severe. The best results come from using expert skiers and planning ahead. I actually compose my pictures with much the same painstaking attention to detail as might Ansel Adams. The mountains, sky, shadows, everything is arranged in the viewfinder as best as I can under the conditions.

In the 1960s sequence cameras were becoming increasingly popular. The most extreme version of the type was the Hulcher, which could be loaded with 100-foot rolls of 2¼x2¼ film,

color or black and white. Able to accommodate long lenses, the Hulcher was a short step away from being a precision motion picture camera. Previously, the motor-driven camera had been used to transport film rapidly, allowing the photographer to keep his eye and hands fixed on picture-making. At times, with a remote mechanism, it puts the photographer in previously inaccessible positions. With

Zimmerman used a Hulcher sequence camera to record those microseconds at the start of the race (below and overleaf).

the advent of the sequence cameras like the Hulcher those milliseconds impossible to grab by even the fastest eye were, at last, captured. Tamed also were those friendly adversaries of sports photography—anticipation and luck.

Like Mark Kauffman, Zimmerman also saw the magic of extreme motion in racing. But while Kauffman played for contrast, the tensions between the bucolic and the frenzied, Zimmerman turned the full force of his attack upon the primary surge as the horses burst out of the starting gate, when the jockeys launch that first push for the rail that often determines the race (page 55). At the Belmont racetrack in New York, "I went to the infield because the sun was right and you can get closer to the horses. I stood on a ladder and the starter even let us build a boom so we could bring the cameras nearer to the animals. The most memorable

thing is the noise. Good Lord, you can't believe the thunder of those hooves and the shouting of the jockeys."

The only picture Zimmerman wanted was of that instant at the start of the race, and only a sequence could assure him of it. As the film whirred through the camera, he caught a flying phalanx of horseflesh screaming from the gate compacted as neatly as a fanned deck of cards (pages 56–57).

The camera paid for itself in a single spectacular photograph advertising graphite shafts for golf clubs (below). What the client wanted was not an illustration of the shaft structure, but a way to draw attention to the product so he could drive home his sales pitch. It was up to Zimmerman to provide the arresting image, so he drew upon an experimental technique he had developed some years before on an editorial story.

"I'm a believer in simple ideas originally executed," Zimmerman

For an ad for a golf club manufacturer (right) Zimmerman adapted a motor drive camera to make stroboscopic pictures in broad daylight without using flash.

One step beyond carbon graphite

says. "Multiple-image stroboscopic pictures had been pioneered by Gjon Mili and Dr. Harold Edgerton about 40 years before. But I don't recall anyone ever doing this kind of a photograph in color." In his front yard, Zimmerman constructed a 16x30-foot backdrop, covered with black flocked paper which absorbs almost all light (regular black seamless paper would have come out gray). Above the black backdrop, he put a sun shield. Zimmerman's

neighbors, had they been in any other town than Los Angeles, with all that exposure to the film industry, might have been nonplussed. Zimmerman used his Hulcher 35mm because its shutter can fire 320 times in a second. He disconnected the film advance mechanism to

allow all the exposures to be cast on a single frame. In this picture of one half second duration—the total elapsed time from the backswing to the completion of follow-through—you can count 160 golf clubs in the picture. Had he needed fewer multiple images, Zimmerman could have achieved the same effect with some simple modifications to his Nikon motor drive (see technical section).

When *Life* wanted a picture story on Oakland

pitcher Vida Blue, who was then having a hot year because of his fierce fastball, Zimmerman got an idea and began tinkering with his 35mm Hulcher again. He removed portions of its circular shutter to allow two separate exposures on a single frame of film. One opening was narrow (1/1500 second) and the other wider (1/15 second). As the shutter revolved, each frame recorded a short exposure and a longer, superimposed one. The picture

(above), which was actually made during a game, caught Blue's rhythm while simultaneously freezing his motion. It captures his flawless form while showing his astonishing speed. There were two special requirements for the picture: Zimmerman used a neutral density filter on the 1/15 opening to keep its exposure consistent with that of the smaller, 1/1500 second opening, and he went to a ballpark where he could count on a dark background caused by an overhanging roof.

The Vida Blue picture has a reportorial quality to it, but Zimmerman often elects to have his technology replace reality with an expressionist statement. Cincinnati outfielder Pete Rose was known for his hustle, a difficult quality to define and an impossible one to hope to photograph during a game. A special shooting would have to be arranged and Rose was happy to cooperate. Zimmerman borrowed a

A double shutter of his own design both froze and blurred pitcher Vida Blue's form.

camera developed by *Life* photographer George Silk, who had experimented with slit cameras in which the focal-plane shutter is stationary and the film is transported past the opening, instead of the shutter snapping open and closed. Such devices had long been employed by racetracks for photofinishes. If the sub-

ject travels at the same relative speed that the film is transported past the focal-plane opening, the image is recorded normally. Any deviation from these relative speeds either stretches out or compacts the subject's image. It was not possible for Zimmerman to just train a camera on Pete Rose while he ran. "We had to have him do a kind of exaggerated dance in order to get on film the kind of flow we wanted," Zimmerman explains. After an afternoon of performing for Zimmerman's cameras, the dogged outfielder articulated in pictures the hustle that has become his signature (page 60).

Zimmerman was asked by an editor at *Sports Illustrated* to do an essay on basketball players Julius Erving (at right), Pete Maravich, Willy Wise and Nate Archibald (far right). Each had a unique attribute that made them star playmakers. With the help of the editor Zimmerman defined what it was, but when it came to interpreting it in pictures he had to rely on his technical skills alone.

Another type of slit camera, manufactured by Panon, does not transport the film past the lens. Instead, as with the Widelux and several other cameras, the lens itself moves. The effect is quite different from all other cameras. In the case of ''Dr. J'' as Erving is known to New York Nets fans, the camera froze the image of his body but recorded his moving arm as he sailed up to lay the ball in the basket. Once the traveling lens had passed over his body, Zimmerman gave Erving a cue to run toward the hoop with the ball clutched in his outstretched hand. For the center section of the picture, the traveling lens saw only a small section of his arm. The basket, as a stationary object, remained tacksharp in the photo. The slithering arm dipping in for a score expresses how deftly Dr. J ''oper-

ates'' on the opposition.

Nate Archibald, a relative midget among the giants of the game, survives on his ability to rise to the occasion with a

deadly outside shot. What Zimmerman wanted to create was an impression of the twisting lower half of Archibald's body zigging and zagging as

he headed up towards the basket. The photographer held the camera vertical and moved it back and forth during the lens sweep, thereby

imparting the contorted image of the lower half of Archibald's body. As he was nearing the basket, Zimmerman steadied the camera. Basket, ball, and the upper torso and head appear undistorted. Seamless paper had to be stretched across the entire background and Zimmerman modified the shutter, slowing it down so as to have more time in which to perform his precise manipulations.

When Zimmerman was assigned to produce an opening illustration to set the mood for a how-to article on tennis by one-time Davis Cup team captain Bill Talbert, he used a multiple-exposure technique. Zimmerman employed the 4x5 camera for the advantages it affords in predetermining the results. The large image area is easier to compose in, and the format accepts Polaroid pack film to guarantee correct image placement as well as test exposure. He placed colored gels over his strobes. The shutter of the camera remained open while a set of switches that one fingers like the keys on a piano fired the lights—bing, bing, bing. To frame the shot of Talbert's serve, Zimmerman later re-exposed the racquet on the same piece of film with the center of the lens masked by a piece of paper that created a reverse vignetting effect (next page).

The repetitive images of Detroit Tiger fastball hurler Denny McLain is the earliest use of the technique described in the golf photograph earlier (pages 58–59). The concept was originally developed for an essay suggested to *Sports Illustrated* but, to Zimmerman's disappointment, not accepted. They graciously gave him back

the rights to the photograph, and it was in his portfolio for some years before being spotted by a bright advertising executive who used it in an ad for Univac. The photograph was made during an actual game, and instead of building a black backdrop, Zimmerman was again able to find a ballpark with a dark enough background from shadows cast by the upper deck of the stands. The technique marks something of a breakthrough in motion photography. While this kind of imagery had been available ever since Dr. Edgerton invented the electronic flash at the Massachusetts Institute of Technology in 1931, it has always required bulky, costly units that required a ready

Zimmerman's use of the Panon slit camera horizontally produced this serpentine shot by Julius Erving (at left) and with the camera on its side showed Nate Archibald uncoiling a shot (at right).

63

power supply. Zimmerman took the technique out of the confines of the studio, did away with the cords, and brought it to bear on unreconstructed events.

An assignment to capture the impact of diver Bob Clotworthy as he struck the water (page 66) required just as much ingenuity. To get sufficient illumination from the right direction, both above and below the water in the Princeton University pool, Zimmerman placed lights in

The 4x5 camera was necessary to align the many complex compositions in this multiple exposure of Bill Talbert.

large aquarium tanks for underwater illumination and more lights on aluminum scaffolding above the water.

With everything in position, Zimmerman then began what proved to be a demanding exercise. He had to go underwater to make the photograph. But he had to move very slowly and hold his breath because any bubbles released by him would interfere with the clarity of Clotworthy's impact upon the stilled water. The photographer could not use a scuba device either, because that also produced bubbles. As Zimmerman slowly slid under the surface, Coles Phinizy, the

On improving delivery of fastballs, etc.

writer on the story, signaled Clotworthy to dive. As soon as he knifed into the water, Zimmerman tripped the shutter and himself shot to the surface, gasping for air. Today, architects design pools with subsurface windows in the walls for observation by coaches or photographers. But there was no such easy route available for Zimmerman then.

During his career Zimmerman has spent a great deal of creative energy on water sports, shooting hydroplanes, water skiers, surfers, sailors and swimmers. One of his frequent companions on such assignments has been longtime friend Coles Phinizy who, in addition to being a *Sports Illustrated* editor who covers boating, is an expert and innovative underwater photographer. Phinizy developed a number of tools for subsurface pictures, including a camera housing Zimmerman used to create the split-level view for a resort area featured in the *Saturday Evening Post* on page 67.

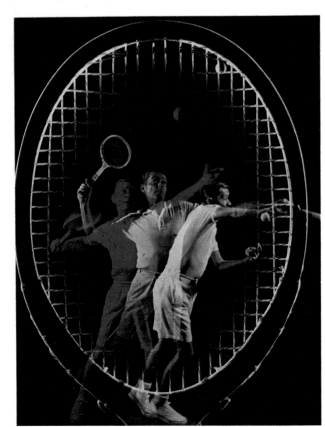

An unsuccessful experiment for an editorial idea eventually became a lucrative advertising photograph.

The problems of
**underwater photog-
raphy are myriad** and
amount to far more than
keeping the camera dry.
As the camera goes
deeper, exposures
change and the colors
shift. The most vexing
problem is the refractive
power of the water itself.
It tends to act as a mag-
nifying lens, which com-
plicates focusing. Phin-
izy's housing solves
many of these problems.
The camera is mounted
in a clear plastic box
whose front window is
set eight inches away
from the lens instead of
the simple inch that is
usual in underwater
housings. As a result,
the camera actually pho-
tographs a well-defined
line of water instead of
an out-of-focus blur. To
the lens is attached a
split filter, the top half of
which is neutral density
to bring exposure for the
portion of the picture
above water down to the

*(left) Zimmerman remained
motionless underwater–sans
scuba gear–so as to catch
the high diver crashing
through the pellucid water.
(right) In this split level
photograph Zimmerman
cleverly hid the problem of
underwater distortion by
adroit placement of the
swimming model.*

By incorporating filters in his multiple shutter Zimmerman's track star seems to trail a rainbow.

level of that underwater. The bottom half is a color-correcting red filter to add the proper amount filtered out of the sunlight by the water. To conceal the disorienting refraction that magnifies the lower part of the man standing in the water, Zimmerman placed his underwater swimmer in such a position as to obscure most of his body and to be at a distance commensurate with the focus above. All of this was accomplished with an implied feeling of casual spontaneity.

A recent improvement by Phinizy corrects the refractions by employing a large reducing lens on the portion of the panel below the water and a half-diopter in front of the camera lens to synchronize focusing. Zimmerman built one of

these devices himself for his cameras. Dolores lost her dining room table to the project, which consumed months of time at considerable expense with no thought that it would ever pay off. Just as he finished it the MGM contract came through, and Zimmerman used the device in a complex poolside photograph of divers entering the water, swimmers above and below, and hotel neatly in focus in the background. Everything was in the proper perspective, focus and color. The problem was that Zimmerman had made it so deceptively natural that when the hotel published the photograph in a brochure, they ran it so small as to be barely decipherable.

Zimmerman eventually loosed his technological bag of tricks upon track

and field events. He used the Panon slit technique upon a shot-putter and a hammer thrower whose gyrations, when distorted by Zimmerman's eyes, captured the extraordinary body torque that provides much of the power behind the toss. For a javelin thrower (preceding page) Zimmerman employed the 35mm Hulcher with its two-slit shutter. Instead of putting neutral density filters over the large slit as he had for Vida Blue, Zimmerman used filters of different colors, thus creating a brilliant parade of blue, green and red effulgences that make the athlete appear to have lanced a rainbow.

Zimmerman built a black backdrop near the track to carry the effect of his filtered multiple shutter.

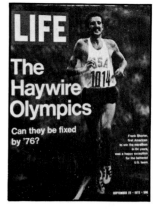

He decided to try the same technique during a race at the University of Oregon in Eugene. The problem was to find a dark enough background with the sun in the right position for rim lighting. "I decided I had to build one up at the end of the track away from the start and finish lines, to avoid blocking the view of the spectators," says Zimmerman. "I explained my notion to track coach Bill Bowerman, but I don't think he fully understood. But he was interested enough to allow us to erect the background and make the pictures."

Conscientious photographers like Zimmerman go to great lengths to try to explain in clear, concise and positive terms the concept of the photograph.

Zimmerman's *Life* cover on gold medal marathon winner Frank Shorter (above) at the 1972 Summer Olympics in Munich was a fluke. *Life* photographers John Dominis and Co Rentmeester flipped a coin with him for positions during the day's events. "Dominis won the spot for this picture, but didn't like his position, so before the start of the race he traded with me," grins Zimmerman. "It's the best deal I ever made during an Olympics."

The pole-vaulter picture at right makes use of one of the most reli-

able devices in sports photography—the scoreboard. Scoreboards not only add graphic values, especially in color, but they often supply punch to a story by spelling out the circumstances of the moment. They epitomize the best in sports photography in that they make a caption unnecessary except for the most literal-minded. Zimmerman's picture is simple. The ecstatic look on the face of the victorious athlete is played against his winning vault measured in meters.

The picture of Soviet gymnast Polina Astakhova on the next page goes back to basics. It was made with a fast 85mm lens using available light. This time there was no complicated technology at work. "To insure that it had the best background available," says Zimmerman, "I positioned myself so as to shoot her when her leaps would carry her into the nearly dark rafters. The light was good and her position was exciting. The only secret is that I had observed her doing her warmup exercises and I was able to anticipate when she would make this leap in her routine."

Anticipation: if anyone wants to develop a lock on photographing the dance of motion, the word is "anticipation." But its key is "preparation."

Zimmerman uses the scoreboard to explain the victorious vaulter's expression in this picture from his last Olympic coverage.

Technical Section

In the realm of sports photography, from a technical standpoint, we are *not* all equal. Most of us with a telephoto or zoom lens can find an advantageous seat at a spectator sport, and get exciting action shots of baseball, horse racing, football, prize fighting or swimming—with good timing and enough light as our allies.

But we must acknowledge a definite difference between the kind of pictures we can shoot and the images of John Zimmerman, Mark Kauffman and Neil Leifer shown in this book, because the latter shoot spectacular and dynamic photographs that require special effort, imagination and equipment. These men must constantly accept the challenge to give an outstanding visual twist to the same sports events we see.

Before detailing the specifics of these photographers' equipment and techniques, let's look at the basic requirements of sports photography that all of us face, whether we are experts or not.

SHOOTING ACTION

It is obvious that fast shutter speeds stop action better than slow ones, and 1/250, 1/500 and 1/1000 second are the primary speeds necessary. Outdoors in sunlight using even the slowest of films such as Kodachrome 25, it is sometimes feasible to shoot at 1/500 second, which will freeze a line of

Using the dark background to limn the balance beam shows the gymnast's flawless form.

football players or a tennis serve. Sometimes a faster film such as High Speed Ektachrome (ASA 160) for color or even Tri-X (ASA 400) for black and white is necessary, especially at football games in the east and north where heavy fall shadows fill the old stadiums after the first quarter. Sharpness is also affected by the direction of the action, covered below.

Another consideration is depth of field, the area of acceptable sharpness from foreground to background. Higher shutter speeds must be matched to wider lens openings, thereby reducing depth of field. If you are 25 feet or more from the subject, however, chances are that even with a medium telephoto lens such as the 135mm, sharpness from the front subjects to the back ones will be suitable. All single-lens reflex (SLR) cameras and most 2¼x2¼ models include a depth of field scale on the lens barrel to which you can refer quickly. There's also a depth of field preview lever on many SLR cameras by which you can stop down the lens while viewing through it and get an approximate depth of field check.

It is "approximate" because the small image you see through the lens makes precise depth of field measurement difficult. By previewing and reference to a depth of field scale, however, you'll know well enough whether the distant players will be in focus or not, and shutter speed-aperture adjustments can be made accordingly. Of course, if you are close enough to the action to use a normal or wide-angle lens, depth of field is far greater than with longer focal lengths. Make comparisons among your own lenses at given distance and aperture settings, and become familiar with the characteristics of each. In this way you can choose and shoot by instinct and experience, and be assured of successful sports pictures.

If you are new at sports and action photography,

shoot a series of pictures at successive shutter speeds, starting with 1/125 second or even slower, and note the differences in prints or projected slides. Such a test will also point up the positive value of blur that occurs with some or all of an image and is often welcome because it symbolizes movement that in some cases frozen figures or objects don't show as well. If you could shoot everything at 1/1000 second (and some cameras offer 1/2000 second) with no limitations on

1/250 F8

1/500 F5.6

1/1000 F4

depth of field or light, it's likely your pictures would soon seem monotonous—so experiment for variety as well as versatility. There are several examples of intentionally blurred photography in the book, such as the track shots by Kauffman on pages 32–33 and 35, and by Zimmerman on page 70.

Fast shutter speeds may be limited indoors with the existing light of a basketball court, for instance, depending on the film you use. A black-and-white film such as Tri-X may allow you to shoot fast enough when rated normally at ASA 400, but if not, you can boost that to ASA 1,200 and have it developed in Acufine or UFG with good quality. High Speed Ektachrome Type B is a good choice for shooting indoor color. Normally it is rated at ASA 125, but Kodak's special ESP-1 processing allows you to boost it to ASA 320 with little color distortion. Lighting at indoor events is unpredictable, and flesh tones may look too warm or too cold, but Type B offers a practical compromise for color, and more speed than negative color films.

DIRECTION OF THE ACTION

Imagine a single football player running toward your camera. His image size increases at a relatively slow rate, and because a figure or object coming toward the camera (or running directly away from it) tends to cover less of a single frame of film in the instant of exposure than one moving *across* the frame, a fairly slow shutter speed can stop its action. That means you can shoot at 1/125 or even 1/60 second, depending on the speed of the action and your distance from it, and get reasonably sharp photographs.

In contrast, if that football player runs diagonally toward you, or across your line of vision, the action progresses over more of the film frame during exposure, and a higher shutter speed, *e.g.*, 1/500 or faster, will be necessary to freeze the image.

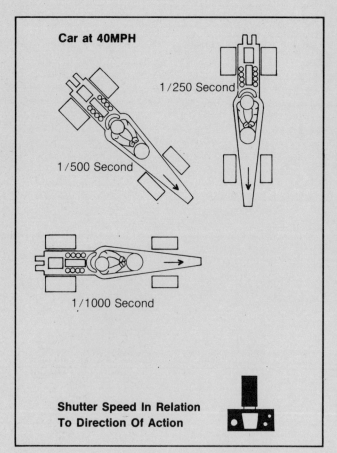

Car at 40MPH

1/250 Second

1/500 Second

1/1000 Second

Shutter Speed In Relation To Direction Of Action

A MATTER OF POSITION

Why shouldn't the triumvirate of Zimmerman, Kauffman and Leifer get good pictures with tons of equipment and press credentials that allow them to shoot from any vantage point they wish? It's a legitimate question, but Kauffman has made some great pictures from the same seats available to all (pages 38–39). Try to get into the most advantageous spot possible. The first row at a football, baseball or basketball game, for instance, is closer than a few rows back, but the elevation of the latter can be useful. In the end zone of a stadium or indoor arena you catch the players striving for a goal or basket, and it may be a good position to take if you have shot, or plan to shoot, from other locations at another time. Again, familiarity with the game involved helps you make choices about camera positions that offer both variety and ample picture opportunities.

Professionals usually *are* privileged to shoot from places that the public can't get to, but that is to be expected because they are working while they watch, and giving valuable publicity to the sports they cover. There are exceptions. Here is Mark Kauffman's account of his prize-winning fight photograph: ''I was in the fourteenth row with a 200mm lens, shooting at about 1/125 second and f/5.6 on Tri-X pushed to ASA 800. I used the natural light of the ring, plus whatever TV light might have been there, and I got some very satisfactory pictures, of which this is the best.

''I think this shows that having a ringside press seat isn't always necessary. For anyone who wants to take pictures at a sports event without a press pass, I suggest: First, try to buy unobstructed seats as close to the action as is appropriate for your lenses. Anticipate the action, and in an exciting

Ask someone to run toward you, then diagonally and perpendicular to camera position, and make a series of tests using four or five shutter speeds. Compare the results. Knowing how the direction of the action influences sharpness, you'll enjoy confidence in choosing shutter speeds, and pleasant surprises in your action shots.

TIMING

An important aspect of every picture in this book was the sense of timing that has been finely developed by all three photographers. Pick a few pictures at random; how effective would they have been if the exposure had been made a second earlier or later? How would composition and story-telling impact have been influenced?

While some situations might have suffered more than others, answers to those questions reveal the extremely refined timing that all three men demonstrate. And how do we parttime sports photographers become more proficient at timing? By awareness of the *peak mo-*

ment, when action is at its most dramatic and exciting and best symbolizes what's happening. As examples, check pages 50–51 of Wilt Chamberlain, or the dogs on pages 4–5, or the steeplechase on pages 26–27. Each photo catches the supreme millisecond when performance of man or animal reaches an apex.

In several ways we can improve our photographic timing to catch similar peak action rather than disappointment in ''near miss'' prints or slides.

1. **Familiarity** with the sport is a must. The more you know about skiing, pole vaulting, football or boat racing, the better prepared you are to take successful pictures. Watching sports on TV is only a beginning. You have to get out there and see the action for yourself while exposing rolls and rolls of film, a lot of which you may discard at first.

2. **Anticipation** of when the action will peak is a direct result of familiarity with the specific sport.

Peak Action
1/125 Second

Descending Action 1/500 Second

Ascending Action 1/1000 Second

Shutter Speed In Relation To Action

TABLE OF SPEEDS FOR ACROSS-THE-FIELD ACTION PARALLEL TO FILM PLANE

| Type of Motion | Distance of Subject from Camera | | |
	25 Feet	50 Feet	100 Feet
Very fast walker . . . (5 mph)	1/125	1/60	1/30
Children running . . .(10 mph)	1/200	1/125	1/60
Good sprinter . . . . (20 mph)	1/400	1/250	1/125
Speed boats, cars . .(30 mph)	1/500	1/400	1/250
Speeding cars . . . . (60 mph)	1/1000	1/500	1/300
Airplanes	—	—	1/500

moment, jump up on your seat. Everyone in front of you will probably have jumped up on theirs as well, and you'll be higher than the person in front of you. If everyone isn't up, be prepared to face the wrath of people behind you. Get a few pictures as fast as you can, and sit down before the seat holder in back throws a punch or a pillow!''

In contrast to Mark Kauffman's telephoto technique at the Rocky Marciano-Archie Moore fight, on pages 84–85 are two of Neil Leifer's photographs of Muhammad Ali. The larger one was made at ringside with a Nikon F and 35mm lens. The insert is one of Leifer's best known shots, made when Ali defeated Sonny Liston in the first round at Lewiston, Maine. Both pictures were made with Ascor strobes placed to backlight the fighters and separate them from the dark background. The camera was a wide-angle Rolleiflex, his favorite for ringside coverage because it synchronizes at fast shutter speeds with strobe and handles easily. Look between Ali's legs and you'll see the other *SI* photographer assigned to the fight, Herb Scharfman, who illustrates why magazines always have two photographers at opposite sides of the ring. This time, Leifer had the best position for the knockdown.

Examples of unusual photographic positions are spotted throughout the book; here are details about a few:

POLE VAULTER BOB SEAGREN
[page 82]

''Shooting from ground level or a little higher might have produced a fairly ordinary picture,'' Neil Leifer states, so he found a spot on a catwalk from where he could capture a unique angle. He shot High Speed Ektachrome in a Hasselblad with 150mm lens at 1/500 second. This camera was chosen because each lens has its own shutter and can be synced with electronic flash (Ascors in this case) at high shutter speeds.

ICE BOATING
[pages 87–89]

Not all of us could persuade an ice boat racer to let us shoot from ahead of the cockpit (adding weight to his craft), but Leifer perched there for the bottom photo on page 87. While he breezed along at more than 100 mph, Leifer shot with a motorized Nikon F and 28mm lens on Kodachrome II at 1/500 second. For the picture above on the same page, he installed a remote Nikon with motor atop the mast, and had the driver ''shoot the roll out.'' His 20mm lens covered everything, and Leifer takes pride that all wires were carefully hidden.

For the going-home mood picture on pages 88–89, Leifer sat in with the skipper as they sailed on Green Lake, Wisconsin. This was also made with the 20mm lens and Kodachrome II.

TELEPHOTO AND ZOOM LENSES

One thinks of normal focal length lenses for all sorts of subjects, and wide-angle lenses for tight places and perspective distortion, but long focal length lenses are often the salvation of sports photographers because they ''reach out'' for images that might not be accessible otherwise.

Says John Zimmerman, ''A long lens may be the only possible way of getting a useful image size from the distance one has to shoot. It may also be used to isolate the subject, allowing the foreground and background to be out of focus. I prefer telephoto lenses over zoom lenses because they generally have faster f/stops and are easier to focus or follow-focus in low light levels. Zoom lenses are useful for the in-between focal lengths, and in some situations where it is possible to keep a subject in focus as it moves—and zoom to maintain proper image size at the same time.

Ski photography is a good example.

''Ski racers come down the course, but because of their different styles and speeds, you don't get exciting pictures at the same spots each time. With an 80–200mm zoom lens, for instance, you can keep the same large image as you begin at 200mm, follow the skier, keep him in focus and zoom back continuously until the racer passes through the 80mm point of action.

''Considering the portability and speed of a lens, a 600mm is about the limit of practicality for me. There are some very fast long telephotos, but they're also very

80-200 Zoom   180mm

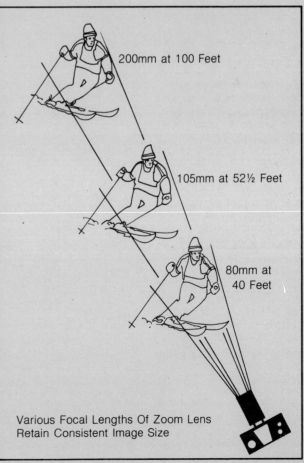

200mm at 100 Feet

105mm at 52½ Feet

80mm at 40 Feet

Various Focal Lengths Of Zoom Lens Retain Consistent Image Size heavy and difficult to run with. There are some lightweight long telephotos, too, but they are almost useless in low light levels. Therefore, in shooting color outdoors, you sacrifice too much mobility with any lens beyond a hand-held 500mm.''

Choosing lenses involves a certain amount of compromise, but there are considerations you should keep in mind:

Speed. If you need maximum apertures, individual lenses, each with its own focal length, are nearly all faster than zoom lenses.

Weight. Individual lenses are in most cases lighter than zoom lenses of related focal length. But several individual lenses, such as 85mm, 105mm and 135mm, will cost and weigh more together than will one zoom lens encompassing that same range and more.

Sharpness. Zoom lenses were once cursed by lack of sharpness; today many of the brands and combinations available are as sharp as individual lenses of any focal length. More glass elements, moving elements, the aid of computers in design and improved manufacturing processes are all involved in providing good zoom lenses in many focal length ranges. A few modern zoom lenses even include a macro mode, which means that by flicking a ring, you can shoot closeups only a few inches from the camera.

TELEPHOTO SHOTS BY LEIFER
[page 81]

This and three other photographs can sum up the usefulness of long lenses. Two cameras shot this situation at the same time. The one on page 81 was made with a 300mm Nikkor f/2.8 lens, a favorite of Leifer's. It is very fast for that focal length. Leifer steadies his Nikon on a unipod, which is one telescoping leg with camera mount on top.

The other camera, seen at the bottom of the picture, was a remote-controlled motorized Nikon with a 17mm

Pentax lens specially fitted to it. It was there to catch the splash as the runners leaped from a puddle on the other side. An assistant fired the bottom camera, making the picture on page 80, as Neil shot with the 300mm.
[pages 90–91]

Here a 400mm Kilfit lens was attached to a Nikon aboard a tripod, reaching out at Fran Tarkington with High Speed Ektachrome pushed one stop. The *Sports Illustrated* lab gave extra development to this film to allow Neil to double its ASA rating.
[page 92]

The *Sports Illustrated* cover was made with an f/5.6 Zeiss 1000mm mirror lens. It is very heavy, but mirror lenses, made with a fixed aperture, are usually lighter because of their special design than conventional telephotos. Most often used is a 500mm mirror lens that weighs only a few pounds. Film was High Speed Ektachrome.
[page 93, top]

Here's an example of results from a Nikkor mirror lens with a fixed f/8 aperture. "It's great for throwing the background out of focus," Leifer says. He uses it on a unipod for mobility. The picture was shot on Kodachrome-X at 1/250 second and f/8. Neil also likes this lens to follow golfers in

tournaments, because he can keep his distance and still get closeup images.

Telephoto lenses that look like cannons are glamorous, perhaps, but unwieldy to hand-hold; and if you're in a crowd or a wind, camera movement is a problem. The average photographer should make a careful comparison between telephotos of individual focal lengths and zoom lenses in various ranges, deciding which to own by the kind of pictures he'll be taking. A short-range zoom (35mm- or 45mm–100mm) is light and versatile indoors or out. Medium-range zooms (50mm- or 60mm to about 135mm) can be excellent for portraits or sports, and longer zooms (70mm- or 80mm–200mm or 250mm) take the place of several telephotos for sports and action. Leifer, Zimmerman and Kauffman, however, are all still partial to telephotos.

LIGHTING WITH FLASH

When you read about numerous and powerful electronic flash units John Zimmerman and Neil Leifer set up in sports arenas, you might envy the pictures they shot. But keep in mind that they faced complex and time-consuming problems while preparing their lighting. There is no way the average photographer can match the quantity of light poured onto an arena by banks of strobes, so what's the answer? Either shoot with the fastest film possible in existing light, or get a camera position close enough to the players so that a portable electronic flash will be effective.

The smallest electronic flash units punch out just enough light to shoot a basketball game from about 20 feet with black-and-white film at perhaps f/3.5, but if your guide number for Kodachrome 25 is 30, forget it. At 10 feet you must shoot at f/2.8, keeping in mind that where there are no close reflective wall surfaces as are found in an average room, exposures must be longer,

i.e., apertures larger, than guide numbers indicate. The same applies to automatic exposure flash units with low light output.

A number of portable, battery-powered electronic flash units made today, however, are stronger (K25 guide numbers of 50 and 75), automatic and reasonably priced. If you shoot with High Speed Ektachrome Daylight rated at ASA 400 with special processing by Kodak or a custom lab, you can cover a lot of players 25 feet away at f/2.8 or f/4. Action is nicely frozen by electronic flash, which recycles in a few seconds and allows you to shoot almost a sequence of action. Ni-cad batteries eliminate replacement costs and penlight or high-energy battery packs have their advantages as well.

Flashcubes and miniature flashbulbs are almost useless for sports unless you are 10 feet or less from a subject, but investment in a portable electronic flash unit pays off in a relatively short time if you do much shooting. Try to use the ambient light indoors first, but if that's not feasible, check the light output of a strobe unit, and buy according to your needs and budget.

Let's examine some of the photographs for further technical background.

HANG GLIDING SKIER
[pages 2–3]

This was part of a story on new ski resorts for *Sports Illustrated.* John Zimmerman shot from a helicopter over Snowbird, Utah, as Jeff Jobey flew over the mountain tops and ski slopes. John was close enough to use a 50mm lens on his motorized Nikon F2, using Kodachrome II at 1/500 second and f/6.3.

DOG RACES
[pages 4–5]

At a Phoenix, Arizona, track John Zimmerman (for *Sports Illustrated*) set up two Ascor 800 series strobes on the track lighting fixtures to illuminate the dogs, and four Ascor 600 series strobes on other light stands aimed at the crowd. Trip cords were suspended over the track to the camera, a Hexacon Supreme with 180mm Sonnar lens. (See diagram.) The camera was one of the first motorized models, now unavailable, and film was old-style Kodachrome 10. John explains, ''I determined that the most dramatic pictures were not of the first dog of the pack, but after he had passed, throwing sand in his wake. You see the following dogs coming through it.''

SULKY AND AUTO
[pages 6–7]

Mark Kauffman set this up in a studio to dramatize racing equipment. ''The pictures had to be composed to emphasize the beauty of different pieces,'' he states, ''so I used a 4x5 view camera and Type B Ektachrome film with floodlights and spotlights very carefully placed. The lens was 135mm (which is about normal on 4x5), and exposure was 1 second at f/11. I used a lot of Polaroid film to check both composition and lighting.'' Today you can use not only a 4x5 Polaroid back on a view camera, but a 3¼x4¼ reducing back that takes all Polaroid pack films. Accessory Polaroid backs are available for the Nikon, Bronica and Kowa Super 66 as well as the Hasselblad.

BINOCULARS
[pages 12–13]

Solving unusual technical problems is normal proce-

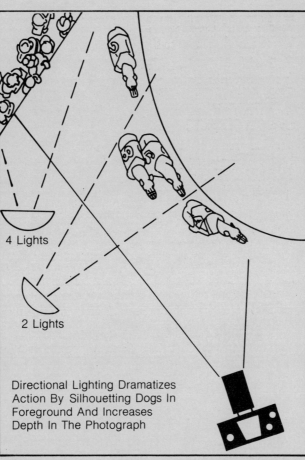

4 Lights

2 Lights

Directional Lighting Dramatizes Action By Silhouetting Dogs In Foreground And Increases Depth In The Photograph

dure for pros, and sports photography has its share of them. Here John Zimmerman had to illustrate how binoculars can enhance a fan's enjoyment of a football game from distant locations. Since the eyes see a single image through a properly adjusted binocular, he took a pair apart and used hàlf of a binocular, adding a cutout form to create a binocular silhouette. The camera and monocular were mounted together and moved as a unit to feature various areas of action; a pair of hands hid the mounting bracket. With a 28mm lens on a Nikon F, John included the magnified view relative to unmagnified surroundings. Film was Anscochrome 64 exposed 1/250 second at f/8.

JAI ALAI
[page 19]

Mark Kauffman explains, ''The top photograph was taken with one strobe light, but by using a slow shutter speed, I got the effect of *two* exposures, one from the flash that froze most of the subject

and the other via the 1/15 second shutter speed that suggested movement for an additional feeling of action. Kodachrome Type A was only ASA 16 when I shot this, but its present speed of ASA 40 would work fine. My Nikon was hand-held, which takes practice. You hold your breath, and squeeze the shutter release just as you would the trigger of a rifle. And you shoot plenty of film to assure yourself frames with minimum camera movement.''

CRICKET
[pages 24–25]

Mark Kauffman shot this game at Oxford University. He says, ''Shooting through leaves frames a picture for added interest. Very often,

depending on how the light hits and reflects off the material used for framing, the color is affected. With a medium telephoto (85mm, 105mm or 135mm) you get the effect of a filter, which in the case of leaves offers a yellow-green tint. Using longer focal lengths such as 300mm, you can shoot through mesh fences or thin foliage and they won't show. I recall covering home plate at Yankee Stadium from behind a wire protective screen with a 400mm lens, and the fence was obliterated. Be sure your lens is as close to the fence as possible and aim through a space.''

STEEPLECHASE
[pages 26–27]

A motorized Foton camera (no longer manufactured) with a specially designed remote control (made by *Life*'s Al Schneider) gave Mark Kauffman one burst—about 8 to 10 frames—as these steeplechase horses leaped the hedge. Speaking about remotely placed equipment, Mark says, ''How well you anticipate the action determines camera location, and in almost every case the photographer must be careful to have permission for a remote setup. The safety of athletes or animals is paramount. Getting the pictures is important, but not at the cost of crippling someone in the process. With that in mind, remote cameras can really get you right into the action.'' Another example taken in the same way appears on pages 30–31.

AIRPLANES
[pages 42–44]

An application of planned blur added excitement to these Zimmerman shots of antique planes in flight for the *Saturday Evening Post*. John mounted a Nikon F with 250-exposure back in front of pilot Frank Tallman with a remote tripper running to Tallman's control stick. Because he wouldn't be in the airplane to shoot, John explained to Tallman what he wanted, and they decided on several maneuvers that would give a maximum roll effect (42–43). Zimmerman set the camera at 1/15 second at f/16 with a neutral density filter on the 28mm lens to tame the light on Ektachrome-X. On a subsequent flight the pilot buzzed an old farmhouse (page 44) which John wanted to be sharp, so the camera was set at 1/500 second at f/16.

HOCKEY
[pages 45–47]

When the New York Rangers management decided there was nothing in the rulebook that prohibited cameras in the goal net, John Zimmerman mounted two motorized Nikons to the framework of one goal for the picture on page 45. Wires were buried under the ice to trip the shutters and fire banks of Ascor strobes installed in each of the arena's four corners. During practice, cameras were protected by pads, and while the game was played, John could activate one camera at a time, or both together. On page 45 old Kodachrome (ASA 10) was exposed at 1/60 second and f/5.6.

For another hockey game featuring Bobby Orr on pages 46–47, John mounted two motorized Nikon Fs with 20mm and 28mm lenses in each goal. He shot this with the 20mm lens at 1/60 second and f/8, again using banks of Ascor strobes to illuminate the action.

BASKETBALL
[pages 48–51]

All these basketball pictures were made during actual games on old Kodachrome with the motorized Hexacon Supreme. About the offbeat shot on page 48 John Zimmerman says, "The attempt was to show the struggle for control of the ball. The pictures were made with electronic flash. I shot through a sheet of glass smeared with Vaseline in a circular pattern, leaving the center clear. The glass was mounted rigidly in place, but I could move the camera behind it for flexibility."

Again Ascor strobes were installed in four corners of the arena for page 49, and John used a remote-controlled Hasselblad EL/M in order to shoot at 1/250 second on Ektachrome-X. He explains that when large strobes are used in unison, they fire at about 1/300 sec-

Nikon F2 With Motor

Motor Drive MD-1 With Battery Pack

ond and may leave an afterglow that mars pictures made at the standard 1/60 second sync speed of a Nikon F. This photo and the one on pages 50–51 were made through a glass backboard, but the latter was shot with a Nikon F on Kodachrome.

SKIING
[pages 52–53]

"The secret to making good ski pictures," states Zimmerman "is to work with expert skiers who can hit a mark you've agreed on. You work as a team. When a fine skier such as Ted Johnson made a slow jump, I could be close enough to use a 50mm lens on a motorized Nikon F at 1/500 second."

The bottom picture on page 53 was shot with the same camera on Kodachrome II at 1/500 second

at f/5.6—from a helicopter. Five skiers were dropped on a peak in the Bugaboo Mountains in Canada. On their first run they created the tracks at right, and John recorded their second trip. The shot on page 54 was made in very early morning from the ground where a helicopter had dropped John, who is a good skier himself.

HORSE RACING
[pages 55–57]

These pictures were part of a story on the first seconds of a horse race, shot from a point close to where the average photographer might have been, using a motorized Nikon F with a 180mm and a 300mm lens and High Speed Ektachrome at 1/500 second and f/6.3.

GOLF SWING
[page 58]

An unusual repetitive image was shot by John Zimmerman with a Hulcher camera firing at approximately 320 frames per second. This photo of the golfer lasted a total of one-half second, and resulted in about 160 sequential images taken against a black background *outdoors*. John suggests that a similar effect, with far fewer images in the series, can be made by the average person with a motorized 35mm camera. First, the black background is essential to prevent objects behind the figure from "bleeding through," and the camera must be mounted on a tripod. Ask your subject to wear dark clothing to minimize overexposure. By keeping your finger on the rewind button (usually on the bottom of the camera), or by activating a multiple exposure lever found on some new model SLR cameras, you can retain a single frame of film in place as repetitive images are recorded on it. If your motorized camera shoots five frames per second, you can expect that number of sequential images for each second of action photographed in this way. The result may seem somewhat meager compared to

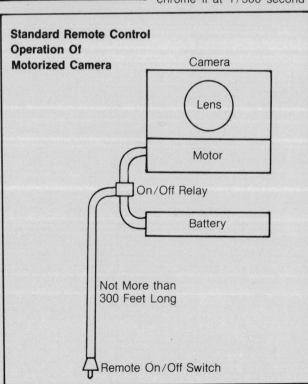

Standard Remote Control Operation Of Motorized Camera

Camera

Lens

Motor

On/Off Relay

Battery

Not More than 300 Feet Long

Remote On/Off Switch

Zimmerman's golfer, but his way is possible if you care to rent a Hulcher camera, which is available in some large cities.

The picture on pages 64–65 was made during a game using the same technique as described above, but the camera was fired more slowly.

Ingenuity and sports photography go hand in hand for the professional who has to solve problems constantly in order to stay ahead of the game. The pun is intended. "The game" is a very serious business to the pro, but fortunately the average photographer can relax, shoot and enjoy without the tension of having to produce outstanding images or else.

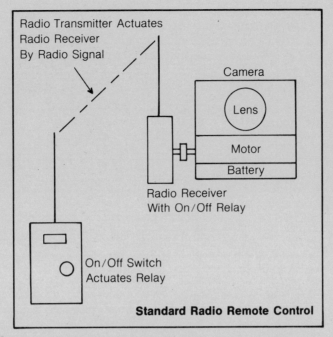

Standard Radio Remote Control

MOTOR-DRIVE CAMERAS

The photographic industry is prolific in manufacturing equipment, accessories and gadgets. Cameras are designed as part of a system that includes everything from microscope adapters to Polaroid backs. Heading the list of "glamor" items are super-telephoto lenses and motor-drive cameras. The latter are either separate motors and battery packs that can be substituted for the standard camera back, or special motorized camera bodies. In any case, a motor-driven camera is very expensive, relatively heavy but extremely helpful in sports and action photography. Prices of these cameras listed on the chart have not been included because they change frequently, but if you will keep in mind that owning a motor doesn't make you an instant professional, let's examine the pros and cons of this valuable equipment.

All the cameras on the chart with the exception of the 2¼x2¼ Hasselblad EL/M are 35mm models to which are attached (or in several brands, built in) electric motors powered by batteries or AC. Here's what they do:

—The motor drive fires the shutter, advances the film and cocks the shutter again faster than you can blink. Some models allow you to shoot semi-automatically, one frame at a time, providing the same functions so you need not remove the camera from your eye to advance the film.

—You can shoot rapid sequence pictures at a rate of 1 to 9 frames per second (f.p.s.) depending on the camera, thereby increasing the opportunity of capturing peak action, if your timing is equal to the machinery in your hands. You begin shooting before the action peaks and continue shooting afterwards, exposing a series of frames that encompass the complete action. From a sequence you can choose the best frame(s) which you might have missed had you been distracted at that moment operating the film ad-

MOTOR DRIVE CAMERAS

Name	Maximum f.p.s.	Weight	Comments
Alpa 11 el	1	2 lbs.	Uses ni-cad batteries.
Canon MD	3	1 lb. 10 oz.	Uses 10AA penlight batteries; this and following two motors all for Canon F-1 cameras.
Canon MF	3.5	1 lb. 7 oz.	Uses 10AA penlight batteries.
Canon High Speed	9	2 lbs. 3 oz.	Uses 20AA penlight batteries; comes as High Speed F-1 camera.
Hulcher Model 112	60 (Unmodified)	3 lbs. 8 oz.	Holds 100 ft. of film, operates on 12V or 24V batteries; accepts Nikon lenses; rotary disc shutter from 1/25 to 1/12,000 second; $1,765 less lens.
Hasselblad EL/M	1	2 lbs. 10 oz. (body only)	Uses ni-cad batteries; motor built-in not add-on.
Leicaflex SL/MOT	4	2 lbs. 4 oz.	Uses 10AA penlight or ni-cad batteries; requires special camera body.
Nikon F2/MD-2	5	1 lb. 5 oz.	10AA or ni-cad batteries; camera needs no modification; provides power rewind.
Nikon F and Photomix FTN	4	1 lb. 5 oz.	Camera body must be fitted for motor drive by Nikon.
Olympus OM-1/MD	5	7.4 oz.	Uses 12AA penlight batteries; cameras without MD designation require modification.
Pentax Spotmatic F	3	2 lbs. 10 oz.	Ni-cad batteries; this is a special motor-drive body with pistol grip.
Topcon Super DM	3	1 lb. 11 oz.	10AA penlight or ni-cad batteries.
Topcon Super DM Auto-Winder	2	9 oz.	4AA penlight batteries; very compact.

vance manually.

—A motor-driven camera may also be placed in a remote location and operated by wire or radio controls at quite a distance from where you are. A number of John Zimmerman's shots of hockey and from a stunt-flying plane were made by remote-controlled 35mm cameras as well as Neil Leifer's top picture on page 87 mentioned before, and his steeplechase picture on page 80.

There are also drawbacks to motor-drive equipment:

—Extra weight and bulk, especially cameras with 250-exposure backs, make shooting more awkward and often so cumbersome you must work from a tripod. Such devices are seductive. Novices tend to get carried away with mechanized clatter as the film whips through the camera in a matter of seconds. It can be inconvenient (and expensive) to reload yards of film every few minutes or so.

—Motors may cost more than the standard camera, and unless you are wealthy or hope to sell some of the pictures you make with motorized equipment, the added weight and complexity may be a luxury not worth the investment. Don't be lured into buying a motor as a status symbol, or you'll have to go without other equipment for which you might have more use.

It may have been obvious as you read this far that at one time or another, motorized photography has been an integral part of the work of all three men in this book. John Zimmerman owns six Nikons with motors, two more with underwater housings and two Hulchers. Neil Leifer uses two Nikon F2s with motors, and Mark Kauffman has used several different models including an older Foton with a spring-wound motor. Each man gained the most of his motorized gear on assign-

ments where making one shot at a time manually might have meant failure. When a magazine is holding four color pages for pictures of a game or race, no excuses are acceptable, and a photographer shoots dozens of rolls of film in many bursts of a motor-driven camera with only one goal: *the* pictures. Thus sports and motors go together. Weight, bulk, inconvenience and expense are all secondary.

In discussing remote-control setups, John Zimmerman comments, ''It becomes routine to place and wire cameras in locations where you can't be yourself. If the distance from camera to tripper is 1,000 feet or more, a relay (to boost electrical power) may be required. There are also problems such as having to adjust exposure when the light changes, weatherproofing the camera in case of rain, and making sure that wires are secured so they won't be accidentally ripped

out by passersby. Wide-angle lenses are generally appropriate for remote camera setups, either because of limited space or because you want to relate subject and background.''

You can learn through practice to advance film and shoot again quickly without moving the camera far from your eye. One frame per second is not unusual via manual operation. Or you can invest in a motorized camera and enjoy the ultimate in sports photography if the expense and extra weight are not handicaps for you. It's comforting to be motorized in many instances, but your skill and visual acuity are more important than how quickly you can shoot.

What Neil Leifer sees with a conventional view of the steeplechase (at right) is not the same as what he gets with a remote-controlled camera (below).

Neil Leifer: An Eye for the Immediate

rapher, "Hey, Strawberry!" and then punctuates the air with three quick jabs—flic, flic, flic. The young photographer beams a wide smile and replies by taking his picture. WHOOOOOOOSH, the arena is bathed in light. Neil Leifer of *Sports Illustrated* has Ali covered again.

An unlikely pair, yet both men fought their way up from hardscrabble origins to achieve success and fame not unaccompanied by colorful controversy. Leifer's rise parallels Ali's. He has photographed all of Ali's major fights going back to 1963 when both were just beginning their professional careers. Born in 1942 in Brooklyn and raised in Manhattan's humble Lower East Side, Leifer grew up a

The scene: A packed arena roaring as Muhammad Ali makes his way down the aisle toward the ring trailed by an entourage of trainers, sycophants, guards and photographers. Climbing the stairs to his corner, he spots a familiar figure at ringside who had been tracking his progress with a Hasselblad. Ali motions to the cherubic red-headed photog-

(left) Leifer was hiding in the rafters when Bob Seagren broke the 17-foot barrier. (below) Leifer neutralizes Ali's "double shuffle" in this outtake, a multiple exposure, from a studio session.

living caricature from the Bowery Boys serials. Leifer was 12 when he was introduced to photography at the Henry Street Settlement House, which offered a two-night-a-week hobby course. A sports fanatic, he spent most of his time playing basketball on hard-top lots and stickball in the streets.

Leifer today tries **to shrug off the popular image that sports journalists are frustrated athletes** by insisting that he still plays a mean game of one-on-one. And despite his ever-widening middle, anyone who has seen him scurrying along the sidelines gets the idea that he's still pretty scrappy, particularly when it comes to playing under the boards. He admits, however, that "in a way we're all frustrated jocks. When you're behind home plate with a 600mm lens, you're batting against Catfish Hunter."

As a boy he was fascinated by the romance of the United States Navy, and as a boy photographer he used to make pictures of the battleships pulling into the Brooklyn Navy Yard across the river from his home. "I'd take the subway out to Floyd Bennett Field, stand on Rockaway Boulevard and photograph the jets coming in. Then I'd go home, develop them in the

By lighting the ring to pick up highlights, Leifer adds drama to these classic poses of Ali over Liston (inset) and Bonavena.

bathroom and make a few prints. That's what I'd do with my weekend."

It wasn't too long before he realized that the photographers got into sports events free, and he began toting his camera, then a Yashicamat, everywhere he went. He witnessed his first heavyweight fight—the Patterson-Johansson 1959 title bout where the champion went down seven times—from a $5 seat in the upper grandstand of Yankee Stadium. He was accompanied by John Iacono, a friend from the settlement house who is now a contract photographer with *Sports Illustrated*. "We were taking pictures anyway," Leifer recalls, "but it wasn't until after the third knockdown that we realized that it was the black guy who was going down."

As an example of the

speed of his rise, by the time of the rematch a year later Leifer had secured a roving press pass in the name of Dell Publications, which had begun using some of his photographs for their one-shot pulp magazines. He got as close as the fifth row press circle. The final Patterson-Johansson match a year later saw Neil Leifer sitting at ringside for

Sports Illustrated.

It became apparent to Leifer's father, a retired postal employee, that his son was not going to enter college and study law or medicine. It seemed inevitable that he was going to follow what they called "a rich man's hobby." To support his photography addiction, Leifer took a job delivering sandwiches for the Stage Delicatessen, a favored eating spot for celebrities just north of the theater district on Seventh Avenue. He worked after school but the hours were flexible enough to allow him to run off to photograph sports. He was a New York Giants football fan. One day while sitting in the stands he noticed that the only people allowed on the field besides the team, the accredited photographers, and the cops, was a group of paraplegics from the Veterans Hospital who were wheeled out before the game and allowed an unobstructed view from near the centerfield wall. He found out what time they arrived and was there waiting the next week. He approached the orderly in charge and, in his politest voice, announced that he would be happy to help wheel the veterans in. It soon became a regular routine during the Giants' home games.

Once inside, **the veterans didn't need much assistance,** so Leifer could pursue his photography. "After a while, when the plays started to come down towards the end zone near us, I'd sort of creep up to the sidelines to get my pictures," he recalls. "I got my first big picture that way, of Alan Ameche scoring the winning touchdown in the 1958 Colts-Giants sudden death overtime."

"As the season wore on it would get cold and

the vets brought a coffee urn. I'd go down to the bench where the guards were and offer them a cup of coffee. I'd chat for a while and then whip out my camera. It made it a little more difficult for them to chase me off the field, and for about ten minutes (about as long it took the coffee to get cold) I would shoot along the bench."

It wasn't too long before the sports photography establishment in New York started to complain about the redheaded tyro and he was summarily banned from many of the sports events in the city. The shutout was so effective that he was reduced to taking a bus to Philadelphia to shoot the Phillies games in order to support his habit. In retrospect, Leifer feels that the blackballing was a boost to his career. "I just didn't like being told that I couldn't take my pictures, and tried all the harder."

Leifer received help from some unexpected quarters. Jack Mara, the owner of the New York Giants, took an occasional cup of coffee at the Stage. One day the owner, Max Asnas, grabbed Mara and complained in his raspy voice, "Hey, this kid takes pictures and your people won't let him in

anymore. Whaddya gonna do about it?'' When Mara got back to his Columbus Circle offices he must have drafted a memo that went through the Giants organization, because shortly afterwards Leifer received a letter notifying him that an entire season's worth of sideline passes were waiting for him at the head office.

Around the corner from the Stage was the *Life* photography studio, and the photographers working there would regularly order out. His Uncle Sammy was the cashier who would make sure that Neil got the run, but at times he regretted it when Leifer would not return for hours.

''After the lunchtime rush I might get an order to take them three cups of coffee,'' says Leifer. ''Tony Triolo (then a *Life* assistant, now a staff photographer at *Sports Illustrated*) would give me a couple of rolls of film as a tip. That was like a two-dollar tip to me.''

''Ralph Morse was always doing those wildly technical production numbers that were fun to watch, and he was the sort of guy who would be happy to explain everything he was doing.'' Leifer hung around the studio and got to meet all of the *Life* and *Sports Illustrated* photographers whose bylines he had so admired. When he heard of an elaborate lighting setup at Madison Square Garden he would go down there ahead of time and watch the photographers install it. He took careful note of where they aimed their lights, of how they wired their units together. In a few years he would be

A Leifer essay on ice-boating in Sports Illustrated

doing the same. When Zimmerman was covering a game he would buy a ticket behind Zimmerman's position to observe how he worked.

In 1960 Leifer desperately wanted to photograph the World Series being held in Pittsburgh. He scrounged a press credential through Dell, and *Sports Illustrated*'s picture editor offered to process his film in order to have a first look at it. For his first big assignment Leifer decided that he had to have a motor drive. His father, who all his life had paid cash for everything, signed for one on credit at a camera store because Neil, at 17, was underage. It came to $450. One of the owners of the Stage stealthily slipped him a $100 loan for expenses. After flying to Pittsburgh, he got a hotel room and spent his first night alone in a strange city. The next day at the ballpark with his roving credential, Leifer was crouching in the aisle near the first base line when, on his first roll of film with the new camera, he caught Yogi Berra being picked off second base. It turned out to be the most significant play of the game. The next day

CHILLY HOT-RODDING ON THE ICE   PHOTOGRAPHS BY NEIL LEIFER

One sail on an iceboat, say those who have tried it, and you are hooked for life. This means, in all likelihood, that Joe Norton, the 16-year-old shown opposite, will spend the rest of his years skidding across frozen lakes at speeds of 50 to 100 mph or more. Iceboating is probably as old as sailboating, but the advent of Dacron sails and space-age metals has given it a new spurt. Today there are more than 3,000 iceboats waiting only for a hard freeze to screech out into lung-searing cold on lakes from New Jersey to Wisconsin. Iceboat classes range from huge two-man A boats, which are 56 feet long, 32 feet across and spread 650 square feet of sail, to the smaller catboat-rigged DN60s, such as that sailed by Joe Norton. The enthusiastic iceboaters who sail them (following pages) number among them many topflight waterborne sailormen like Olympian Harry (Bud) Melges and at least one topflight sailorwoman.

30

Leading two rivals, Bill Perrigo whips across Green Lake at a mile a minute.

Leifer provides a romantic
finish to a day of ice boating by photographing them
against a colorful sunset.

Leifer shot black and white and then returned to New York. *Sports Illustrated* picked up one black and white photo for a full page, paying $150, and used the color of Berra for a page, paying $300. Two weeks later he received his check from the magazine and proudly signed it over to the camera store owner to wipe out his father's debt.

Publication in **the magazine was a foothold but still far from a career.** The working press kept the pressure on. Walter looss, Jr., a *Sports Illustrated* photographer a year younger than Leifer, traveled the same route. "I first noticed Neil at a New York Titans football game, and said to myself, 'Hey, there's a young punk just like me. What's he doing here?' I felt more confident seeing him out there. He was his own man even then—very gutsy.

"My dad got us together. I wanted to show Neil my portfolio, so we arranged to meet in the lobby of the Time-Life Building underneath the painting. It was romance at first sight. I was 16 and Neil 17. He had been published in Dell. I idolized him.

"Those were rough years. We'd be shooting through the screen behind home plate and the press photographers up in the gallery with those Big Berthas would spot us. They kept screaming for us to get our asses

out of there with those little cameras. They would send the ushers down to chase us out. And we paid for those seats!"

The resentment from his older rivals was due to Leifer's spirited enthusiasm, aggressiveness and in no small part to his skillful use of the 35mm single-lens reflex that had yet to invade newspaper photojournalism. The assignments began to come with more regularity. *Sports Illustrated* sent Leifer, at the age of 19, along with looss, to cover the World Series in Los Angeles in 1962. "Nobody believed we worked for the magazine," recalls looss. "We had to have the stringer come out to the airport to rent a car for us. Herbie Scharfman (a veteran of *Sports Illustrated* and the Dodgers' team photographer) went into shock. I don't think he's fully recovered yet."

In 1965 Leifer was put on contract with the magazine. If there was grudging acceptance along with official accreditation, it immediately turned into hearty admiration upon the publication of Leifer's pictures of an Ali triumphant over Sonny Liston (inset page 85) that year, followed by another picture of Ali over Oscar Bonavena (pages 84–85), which amount to two of the finest victory statements in boxing. "In the old days you could just hang four lights and shoot at f/8. Today you add drama by

Normally when doing an essay on a quarterback Leifer would position himself to look in his subject's face. But he reversed his thought here, dropped back and concentrated on the opposition linemen who much better illustrate the perilous position of a quarterback.

having a backlight on the shoulders, which is especially effective with black fighters in making them stand out.''

Leifer's approach to boxing is markedly different from Kauffman's. Both are consummate professional journalists, but each tells his stories with different accents. Kauffman's (pages 38–39) is soft, evocative, subtle in its delivery. The picture's heartrending emotions slowly overtake the viewer. Leifer's voice is bright, immediate, bold in its articulation. The picture's sensationalism makes a swift impact on the viewer. Kauffman's roots are those of a photo essayist in the *Life* tradition who would take the longer, more cerebral approach to a story. *Sports Illustrated* in its early days was of that mold too, but in the early sixties the magazine became faster, more reactive to the week's events. Leifer is a product of the second generation of *Sports Illustrated*

photography. He makes his point in one quick audacious stroke, typically telling a story with a classic pose of victor over vanquished.

Leifer prepares for a fight by first going through his old photographs: ''If I shot in that arena before I look at my lighting, try to figure out a way to do it differently this time. Going back over your pictures from time to time is more important than to keep shooting. Long after a story has run I go back through the slide boxes to see which positions and lenses worked and which didn't. Those that work I analyze to see how they could have been made better.''

Leifer picks his spot near a neutral corner with his back to the TV lights. With a medium telephoto he has a good line to both fighters' corners, and good access to 75 percent of the ring. ''Still, I don't get as many punches as I should, and that's be-

cause I use a Rollei, and lately a Hasselblad, on boxing. That's the only time I use that equipment all year. To get used to it again I sometimes shoot the preliminary events with Polaroid film to kind of warm up. Yet I don't perform as well as I should. Ideally, I'd like to be able to shoot another fight the week before to prepare myself. Fortunately, the magazine wants more than the knockout punch.

"**W**hen George Foreman hit the canvas in Zaire** it was an earth-shaking event in sports. The excitement of a heavyweight championship fight is terrific. And in that atmosphere a lot can go wrong. I've seen old pros reload their cameras with the same film. To prevent accidents I tape my exposure to the aperture ring so it won't slide on me. I tape the sync cord in the socket. Just about everything that moves, I tape. I end up with a very heavy Instamatic that focuses.''

It's a long way from the stifling streets of Manhattan to the barren expanse of a frozen lake in Wisconsin, but Leifer accepted one of his finest challenges when he undertook an essay on ice boating (pages 87–89). It gracefully combines imaginative positioning of the camera (the opener), exciting action (the spread), and sensitive emotion (the ender, pages 88–89). ''My aim was to put the

reader in a place where he would most likely never be.'' Few hope to be nailed to the mast of a spindly iceboat knifing through the wind at 100 mph like Leifer's remote-controlled Nikon. For one series of pictures Leifer perched on the bow facing back towards the skipper. ''I had no idea how fast we were going, although I later learned it got as high as 130 mph. My only concern was to keep the horizon level. After I finished the essay they invited me back to take a lesson. I never took the boat past 70 because I was scared stiff. And cold! I never noticed before the little chips of ice that stream over you, cutting into your face. I guess that's why I remember that I often had to clean my lens.''

''If I had to cover news all the time I'd quickly go stale. If you continually look for the big play all the time, eventually you will find it. And when you've got that, what more can you do? You go through a psychological letdown. To avoid that, I constantly try to do different things like essays, features and personality profiles.''

Some of Leifer's finest work has been done in football, on which he offers some advice: ''Every photographer should have a good working knowledge of the game. Whether it's high school football or the pros, all teams have characteristics that you should be ready to key on. Does the quarterback bark out his signals? Maybe there's a good portrait there. Is the cold a factor in the game? Maybe you should go to the other sidelines to backlight their frozen breath. Is it a passing situation? Who's the favorite target?

Sports Illustrated

SEPTEMBER 12, 1966   40 CENTS

CHICAGO'S CHALLENGING BEARS
BUKICH HANDS OFF TO SAYERS

Maybe you should track him.

"I always look for stories within the game. Last year I spent eight games observing the centers for a big essay. The Bob Brown story (pages 93–96) was done over a period of five games—one half of one game was spent just watching his wife and little boy in the stands watch him play football."

More than other photographers, those who specialize in sports can justify their indulgence in the tantalizing array of equipment constantly being churned out by the manufacturers. Since their subjects always operate within a given set of guidelines, new lenses offer a different perspective to an old subject. Leifer delighted in a new 400mm lens Nikon introduced last year and used it all season.

Some years ago he conceived the idea of presenting the reader with a sense of the huddle. He rigged a remote camera with two small strobes mounted on a board that he placed in the middle of the huddle as they assembled. When the huddle broke, he quickly pulled the device off the field from the sidelines. Leifer pushed the idea to the point of actually having a cover dummied up even before he had shot the picture. With the encouragement of picture editor George Bloodgood he finally got the opportunity to use the device on a story about the Arkansas Razorbacks. The coach was considerate of a senior who didn't regularly play and always sent him into the pregame huddle—the one

Leifer was photographing. When Leifer got back to New York and was proudly showing the pictures in the screening room one of the editors started counting heads and came up with 12. A chagrined Leifer went off to try it another week, but this time he made sure there were only the regulation 11 heads in the huddle. He finally got his picture, but it would never run. Leifer learned firsthand about a frustrating psychological quirk common to all editors: Good ideas pale fast if not published soon. The concept of the picture had become shopworn after weeks of delay. In spite of Leifer's delivery of the picture he had promised, the editors had by then lost their enthusiasm for it. "Probably it would have been better to sneak up on them with the picture," Leifer muses. "I get laughed out of the building every time I bring it up, but I haven't given up on the idea yet."

Leifer uses a motor drive almost always. The reason, he simply states, is "percentage."

"Assume I'm at the Super Bowl, and the game-winning touchdown is about to be made from the one-yard line. The fullback comes charging through, springs off his guard's back, leaps 20 feet in the air and the game is won. I got the picture. All of a sudden he hits the linebacker and fumbles. The story has changed that quick. A second ago I did precisely what I was supposed to do, but in the seconds it takes for me to advance the film *the* picture has been lost. The motor drive reduces the number of times you have a bad day."

Leifer is distressed by the pejorative image of the sports photographer as "a typical American paparazzo with 17 Nikons and mud on his shoes." An open but sensitive young man, he lives quietly in the Long Island suburbs with his wife of 10 years, Renae, and their two children, Jodi, 8, and Corey, 4. In spite of all of his success in the medium he still has the wide-eyed enthusiasm of the sandwich boy sitting in the shadows of a Kauffman

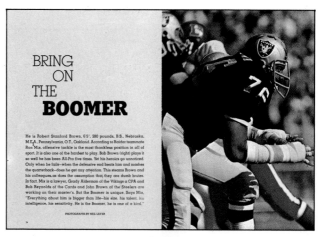

BRING ON THE BOOMER

He is Robert Stanford Brown, 6'5", 280 pounds, B.S., Nebraska, M.F.A., Pennsylvania, O.T., Oakland. According to Raider teammate Ron Mix, offensive tackle is the most thankless position in all of sport. It is also one of the hardest to play. Bob Brown (right) plays it so well he has been All-Pro five times. Yet his heroics go unnoticed. Only when he fails—when the defensive end beats him and mashes the quarterback—does he get any attention. This steams Brown and his colleagues, as does the assumption that, they are dumb brutes. In fact, Mix is a lawyer, Grady Alderman of the Vikings a CPA and Bob Reynolds of the Cards and John Brown of the Steelers are working on their master's. But the Boomer is unique. Says Mix, "Everything about him is bigger than life—his size, his talent, his intelligence, his sensitivity. He is the Boomer, he is one of a kind."

PHOTOGRAPHS BY NEIL LEIFER

or a Zimmerman. "I'm more interested in what makes those guys tick than in what their pictures look like. Mark's personal approach fascinates me. Every time he puts his hand out he makes friends for the magazine. Their personalities probably didn't make their pictures any better, but it sure made it a lot easier for them to work, and for those who followed them, like me. I was aggressive and rough when I started out but I like to think that I've matured since then. The first time I worked a horse race at Santa Anita I met an old gentleman who was a judge. When he heard that I was from *Sports Illustrated* he inquired about Kauffman and Zimmerman. He first met them

Brown exults on the bench after a winning performance.

when they were in high school. Bach used to send them out to the track in a coat and tie. The old man never forgot that, and had been following their careers ever since. That incident made a deep impression on me. Those guys exude class."

All three photographers are in a special class. They have an effortless facility with the technology, a prerequisite for shooting the world of motion, which they combine with agile reflexes guided by an acute eye. And what puts them in a class by themselves is their individual imprint on their pictures: Kauffman's sensitivity, Zimmerman's innovation, Leifer's boldness. The statements of Kauffman, Zimmerman and Leifer are inescapable, vivid, and often better than a ringside seat.

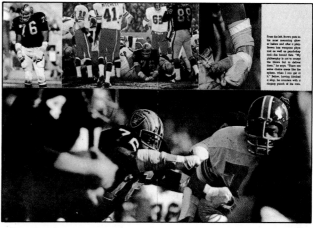

Leifer shows the enormity
of his subject by contrasting him with the coaches.

96